Linden Lea

'Ithin the woodlands, flow'ry gleaded,
By the woak tree's mossy moot,
The sheenen grass-bleades, timber sheaded,
Now do quiver under voot:
An' birds do whissle auver head,
An' water's bubblen in its bed,
An' there vor me the apple tree
Do lean down low in Linden Lea.

When leaves that leatley wer-a-springen
Now do feade 'ithin the copse,
An' painted birds do hush their zingen
Up upon the timber's tops:
An' brown-leav'd fruit's a-turnen red,
In cloudless zunsheen, auver head,
Wi' fruit vor me, the apple tree
Do lean down low in Linden Lea.

Let other vo'k meake money vaster
In the air o'dark-room'd towns,
I don't dread a peevish measter:
Though noo man do heed my frowns.
I be free to goo abrode
Or teake agean my hwomeward road
To where, vor me, the apple tree
Do lean down low in Linden Lea

WILLIAM BARNES

☐ BEACHES 6-7
■ WALK 8-15
■ CYCLE....................16-24
■ KAYAK....................25-27
■ MUSEUMS GALLERIES...28-36

■ ARTISTS WRITERS..........37-42
■ HISTORY..................43-68
■ FOLKLORE.................69-79
■ EXPLORE.................80-114
■ CHURCHES...............115-121

■ SHERBORN

■ The Blackmore Vale

■ Sutton Bingham

■ Benjamin Jesty

■ The Woodwose

Dors Dialec

Pilsdon Pen ■

■ Skimmity Riding ■

Cures and ■ Curses ■

The Ooser ■

The Screaming Skull ■

The Everlasting Stone ■

The Holy Well ■

Whitchurch

Eggardon and Hand ■ Hillfort

The Cross ■ ■ The Monks Way

Along the Lim ■

James Whistler

■ Canonicorum

Tacky's Rebellion

Lysco Chap

The Town Mill ■

■ LYME REGIS

Symondsbury Cycle ■

■ Valley of the Stones

■ The Count Museum

■ Golden Cap ■

Chideock ■

■ BRIDPORT

Maumbury ■ Rings

The Philpott Museum

Bridport ■ Rope Industry

The Dorset Pilgrims

DORCHESTER ■

The K Museu

■ Monmouth Rebellion

Bridport ■ Flea market

The Hardy ■ ■ Monument

Bronkham Hill

Hardy Country

Poundl

■ The Undercliff

The Viking Massacre ■

John Const

■ The Knoll

Maiden Castle ■

George III ■

■ Do Deco

ABBOTSBURY ■

■ WEYMO

The ■ Sub-Tropical Gardens

J. Mead Faukener

Sandsfoot ■ Castle

Plague! ■

■ Portlan Harbour

Tout Quarry ■

The Dorset Mermaid ■

The Easton ■ Massacre Rabbit! ■

■ Th Jailho Cafe

Portland ■ Bill

Portla Muse

■ The Isle Portland

The Byzant

The Abbey
Museum

SHAFTESBURY

Goldhill
Museum

Hambledon
Hill

The God
of Love

The Damory
Oak

The Lost
Mansion

STURMINSTER
NEWTON

Sturminster
Mill

Buttony

BLANDFORD
FORUM

The Fire
of Blandford

The Dorset
Clubmen

The Dorset
Cursus

The Mizmaze

Knowlton

Milton
Abbas

Horton
Tower

North Dorset
Trailway

Wimborne
Minster

Roman
Dorset

Augustus
John

Frankenstein's
Mother

The Chained
Library

T. E. Lawrence

POOLE

Russell-Cotes
Museum

Across the
Heathland
Martyrs

Wareham

Poole
Museum

BOURNEMOUTH

Bovington
Tank Museum

Exploring
Poole Harbour

Bournemouth
Esplanade

Bere
Regis

Middletown

Swanage
Ephemera

Sculpture by
the Lakes

J. M.W
Turner

Hingstead
Clifftops

Clavell
Tower

Durleston
Castle

Worbarrow
Bay

Hingstead to
Lulworth

The Dorset
Quarries

Kimmeridge
Shale

Wreck of
the Halsewell

St Ahelm's
Head

Insider's Dorset is the kind of book I would like to find if I was a visitor to Dorset.

It is a collection of the less obvious which will hopefully make your visit more rewarding.

The contents are all the products of my own experiences.

I've walked the walks, explored the byways, cycled the cycle routes and photographed the views.

Most importantly, I've thoroughly enjoyed myself. I hope you do too!

Ian Dicks

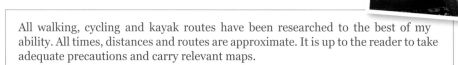

Dedicated to the
memory of Geoffrey Tizzard
A true man of Dorset
1949-2015

All walking, cycling and kayak routes have been researched to the best of my ability. All times, distances and routes are approximate. It is up to the reader to take adequate precautions and carry relevant maps.

INSIDER'S DORSET by Ian Dicks
Text and illustration copyright
IAN DICKS 2016
The right of Ian Dicks to be identified as the author and designer
of this work has been asserted by him in accordance with the Copyrights and Patents Act 1988
All rights reserved
A catalogue record of this book is available from the British Library
ISBN 978-0-9935028-0-4

Insider's
Dorset

Ian Dicks

Dorset's Beaches

Weymouth

LYME REGIS The town beach consists mainly of sloping pebbles with sand near to the picturesque Cobb Harbour. To the east is the quieter Church Beach, pebbly with sand at low tide. Beyond the Cobb is the wilder Monmouth Beach. The area is a fossil hunter's paradise.

CHARMOUTH The beach lying a quarter of a mile from the village centre is a mix of shingle and sand. There are fossils to hunt as well as rock pools to explore at low tide. The Heritage Centre gives you a fascinating insight into the area and has a cafe.

SEATOWN A peaceful beach with shingle that shelves quite steeply.

EYPE Shingle beach with a backdrop of Golden Cap, Dorset's highest headland.

WEST BAY Two wide, shingle beaches, East Beach and West Beach which is divided by a lively harbour.

BURTON BRADSTOCK A long sandy beach overlooked by cliffs and farmland.

CHESIL BEACH An 18-mile bank of pebbles that is one of the wonders of the natural world.

Currents and a steeply shelving beach

Durdle Doo

make bathing unsafe. Behind it lies the Fleet, an enclosed area of brackish

Weston Mouth nouth · Branscombe · Beer · Seaton · Lyme Regis · Charmouth · West Bay · Seatown · Chesil · Weymouth · Ringstedd · Durdle Door · Kimmeridge · Lulworth Cove · Studland · Swanage · Bournemouth

water designated an area of special scientific interest. The beach pebbles are graded by the currents; from gravel in the west to large pebbles in the east. In previous centuries fishermen used this phenomenon to gauge exactly where on the coast they had landed.

CHURCH OPE A peaceful spot presided over by the remains of Rufus Castle and the ruins of Portland's first church. The only real beach on Portland and which can only be reached on foot. No facilities except a toilet.

WEYMOUTH The beach is a sweeping crescent of fine sand unequalled for sand castles. The shallows are perfect for toddlers. It is the quintessential English resort with donkeys, swing boats, candy floss and a wide esplanade.

RINGSTEAD A peaceful unspoilt beach with a wide curve of shingle beach and safe shallows. Distant views of Portland and walks on the chalk cliffs.

DURDLE DOOR Two long shingle beaches are separated by the rock outcrop of Durdle Door itself. Access is on foot down a long path from the car park.

LULWORTH COVE Lulworth has become synonymous with the Purbecks. The beach forms an almost full circle broken by just a narrow entrance. It is mostly shingle and child friendly.

KIMMERIDGE A wide cove backed by low cliffs. Rocky outcrops make it one of the best places for rock pooling. It is a popular destination for divers. There is a marine centre and WC but no cafe.

STUDLAND A long stretch of sandy beach owned by the National Trust. Superb for children, so crowded in high season.

SWANAGE Like Weymouth, it is a traditional holiday resort. With a wide esplanade fronted by a sandy beach perfect for children.

BOURNEMOUTH The sandy beach stretches all the way to Poole. It is backed by a wide car-free promenade with the many kiosks and snack bars and a pier at its centre.

Kimmeridge

Worbarrow Bay

You will experience some of the best of the Purbecks on this walk. It begins at Povington car park. If you're feeling lazy, step no further–this is about as good a picnic spot as you can get.

The walk follows the chalk ridge through the military range to Flowers Barrow, the remains of an Iron Age hill fort that clings precariously to the cliff edge. From its ramparts you look down upon the sweep of Worbarrow Bay, ending in the tiny peninsula of Worbarrow Tout. The bay is a favourite spot for passing yachts to drop anchor as the beach is only accessible by foot or sea. A detour takes you to the fascinating deserted village of Tyneham.

Alternately you can continue along the cliff edge for stunning views in all directions. After dropping down into the valley, climb up again to follow the ridge back to the car park.

This walk forms part of the Lulworth Range Walks-access varies
Distance: 7 miles
Tyneham circuit 4.5 miles
OS Explorer OL15

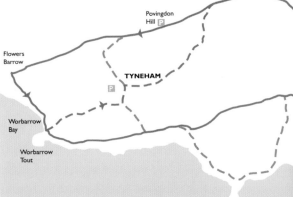

Golden Cap

Golden Cap is one of the highest points on the Dorset coastline and dominates the view both east from Lyme Regis, and west from West Bay. It is Dorset's very own version of Ayers Rock, adopting a myriad of hues depending on the weather conditions and time of day.

Reaching the top is not the struggle you might imagine if you follow the route shown.

The six-mile walk begins at the National Trust car park in Langdon Wood and is clearly signposted. As well as climbing to the summit of Golden Cap, the walk passes the ruined church of St Gabriel. This marks the site of the lost village of Stanton St Gabriel abandoned when the coach road moved inland.

6 miles
Map OS Explorer OL15

The ruins of St Gabriel's church

The walk begins at Milton Abbas, a picturesque village created in 1780 on the whim of the lord of the manor. The village of Middleton happened to spoil his view so he had it demolished moving the villagers out of sight into a double row of cottages around the corner, now the village of Milton Abbas.

The route takes you past Milton Abbey and school and then passes what must be one of the most idyllically situated school playing fields in England. (see p.87)

A long climb brings you to the brow of Bulbarrow Hill, where you are rewarded with incredible views inland over the Blackmore Vale.

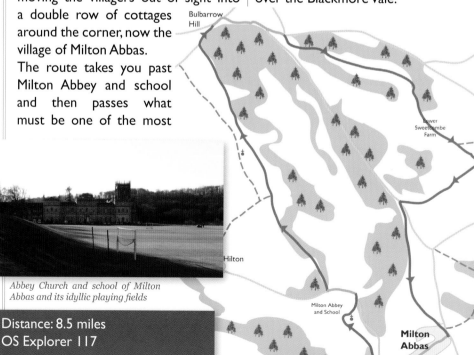

Abbey Church and school of Milton Abbas and its idyllic playing fields

Distance: 8.5 miles
OS Explorer 117

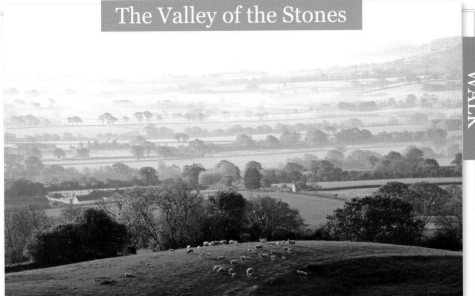

This route passes through three tranquil villages hidden in the softly folding chalk escarpments of the Bride Valley. They form part of a hidden Dorset that is ignored by the crowds rushing seawards along the A35.

The route climbs to the ridge high above the valley, giving level walking and pastoral views. A slight detour takes you to the Valley of the Stones Nature Reserve, considered to be one of the finest examples of a sarsen stone boulder train found in Britain. Conditions at the end of the last Ice Age caused sandstone on top of the chalk hilltops to fragment, slump and scatter downhill. There is evidence that the site was used as an ancient 'quarry' with stones being taken from the area for use at local megalithic sites such as the stone circle which this walk passes.

Litton Cheney

A35

Long Bredy

To Dorchester

Little Bredy

Valley of the Stones Nature reserve

stone circle

stance: 9 miles approx.
S Explorer OL15

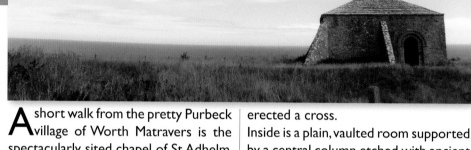

A short walk from the pretty Purbeck village of Worth Matravers is the spectacularly sited chapel of St Adhelm, clinging like a limpet to the clifftop high above the boiling surf.

The chapel has stood in this exposed

Ancient graffiti

position for a 1,000 years, its true purpose lost in anquity. It probably combined the spiritual and practical by functioning as a beacon for ships with a brazier situated at the apex of the roof where the Victorians later

erected a cross.

Inside is a plain, vaulted room supported by a central column etched with ancient graffiti. At Whitsuntide local girls would dance in the ribbon-bedecked interior, dropping pins into ancient cavities in the central column to bring luck.

From here you can see for miles along the Purbecks, views shared by the Coastwatch station close by, which is also worth a visit.

Worth
Matravers

St Adhelm's
Chapel

Distance: 5.5 miles
OS Explorer OL 15

Middle Mill

This walk can be completed in a morning whilst still leaving time for an afternoon on the beach.

It begins at Lyme Regis Town Mill and follows the River Lim, first by road, then by footpath along the old pack horse trail past Middle Mill. In fact travel by pack horse was the only way into Lyme except by sea until the 18thC. The route continues through fields and along footpaths eventually passing Rhode Hill House. This was once the home of Alban Woodroffe, Lyme's great benefactor.

Further on you are treated to an unexpected view of a viaduct of monumental proportions. This is Cannington Railway Viaduct, built in 1903 to carry the Lyme branch line from Axminster. It was the first viaduct to be built completely from concrete rather than brick. Like its classical Roman predecessors, it now stands as a derelict symbol of another age sold by the railways for the grand sum of a penny. (See p.89)

The route returns through leafy glades by the Lim.

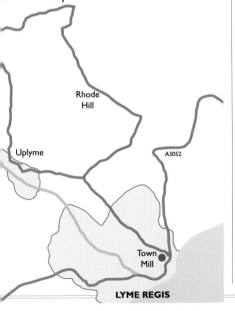

Rhode Hill

Uplyme

A3052

Town Mill

LYME REGIS

Distance: 6 miles
OS Explorer 116

The Dorset Cursus

Jim Champion

Course of the Cursus seen from Martin Down

Around 3,000 years ago, at the time of the construction of Stonehenge, the men of North Dorset built their own impressive monument, the Dorset Cursus.

It consisted of parallel chalk banks five feet high, six feet wide, spaced 300 feet apart and flanked by deep ditches. It snaked across the rolling downland of Cranborne Chase for six and a quarter miles and took half-a-million man hours to construct.

Its earth and chalk construction, though, proved less durable than stone, so that while Stonehenge is still very much in evidence, most of the Cursus has long since disappeared beneath the plough. What is known results from aerial photography and geophysical surveys and shows it stretched between Bottlebush Down and Martin Down. From Martin Down Nature Reserve it takes just a little imagination to conjure those gleaming banks of white chalk stretching to the far horizon.

Theories about the Cursus' construction abound from a processional way to a some kind of Neolithic racecourse.

Martin Down and along Brokerly Ditch

This walk takes you across Martin Down Nature Reserve and along Brokerley Ditch, a bank and ditch dating from the Bronze Age built to mark territorial boundaries. The earthwork was enlarged after the Romans left as a defensive barrier against the invading Saxons.

Distance: 7 mls approx.

OS Explorer OL22

Situated near to Bridport, Eggardon Hill is one of the highest inland points in Dorset, and the views will make you feel lord of all you see.

The hill is less well known than Maiden Castle near Dorchester. Being much higher makes Eggardon Hill much more impressive. The crumpled green ramparts rise and fall in green folds, and, like Maiden Castle, once defied the might of Rome. The route linking the chalk hills is an ancient one and is lined with barrows of the Iron Age tribes, who once made these fortifications their home. Nowadays, invaders are mostly of the waggy variety as it a favourite haunt of dog walkers. It's also a great location for kite flying.

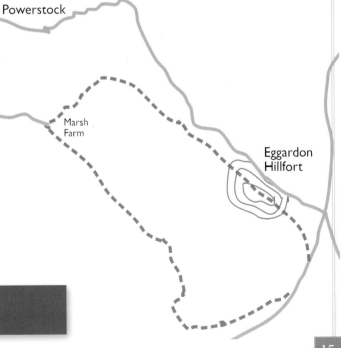

Powerstock

Marsh Farm

Eggardon Hillfort

Distance: 4 miles
OS Explorer OL15

15

T his ride encompasses bridleways, quiet lanes, inspiring views, and a mysterious standing stone.

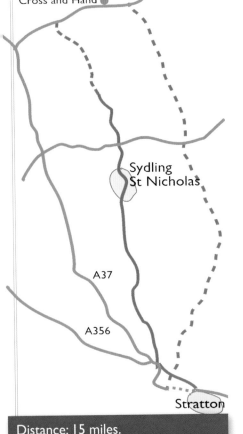

Cross and Hand

Sydling St Nicholas

A37

A356

Stratton

Distance: 15 miles.
OS Explorer 117

Beginning at Stratton, a pretty village with a green and a pub, you negotiate a short stretch of the busy A37 along a thoughtfully placed cycle path.

Take great care crossing the road to the bridleway on the opposite side.

The route is easy to follow and has several surprises such as the rough-hewn stone cross and bench hiding in the undergrowth. The cross was erected in celebration of the Millennium and marks the site of a much older one that once stood on the ancient route connecting the Abbey of Abbotsbury to Cerne Abbey.

Further along the bridleway stands another poignant memorial, a cairn of flints, raised in memory of a woman named Harriet Tory who died at the age of 37.

Leaving the bridleway and turning left on to tarmac, you soon pass the Cross and Hand a mysterious standing stone. It is referred to by Thomas Hardy in *Tess of the D'Urbervilles*. Further along the road a bridleway takes you downhill to the sleepy unspoilt village of Sydling St Nicholas complete with welcoming pub. From there a quiet lane returns you to Stratton.

The North Dorset Trailway is an inspired piece of community planning which has converted the route of a disused railway line to provide 16 miles of safe, traffic-free cycling or walking.

At the moment it runs from Sturminster via Blandford Forum to Spetisbury. It forms a focus for a number of walking and cycling routes that loop from it which can be found on the North Dorset Trailway leaflet.

Winterborne Clenstone's church among the fields

This ride, which starts at Winterborne Kingstone, takes in a trio of Winterbornes before turning through gently rolling countryside and wide skies and on to a short stretch of the trailway.

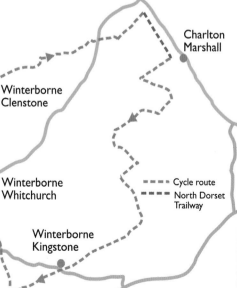

Charlton Marshall

Winterborne Clenstone

Winterborne Whitchurch

Winterborne Kingstone

- - - - Cycle route
▬▬▬▬ North Dorset Trailway

Distance: 17 miles.
OS Explorer 117

Ford over the Frome

This off-road ride starts from Moreton village, the burial place of Lawrence of Arabia. (The tearoom uses the bier that carried his coffin for its display of cakes!)

Crossing a picturesque ford (with a bridge should you want to keep dry...) it then scoots along a firm, level cinder track to Turner's Puddle where stands a small neglected church. The bells, dating from the 14thC, were stolen in the 1950s but mysteriously reappeared on a Christmas Eve, covered in mud at the door of the farm. A note was attached stating, somewhat enigmatically...

'Sorry, Christmas...'
The rest of the trip is along quiet lanes and over heathland with sightings of deer if you're lucky.

Distance: 19 miles
OS Explorer OL15

Distant view of Colmer's Hill

Beginning at the charming village of Symondsbury, this ride is brought to you courtesy of the Symondsbury Estate who, with an admirable altruistic gesture, have created a free waymarked cycle-route around the estate.

It is a short ride but a fun introduction

Sunken lane

to offroad cycling for all the family, with a landscape ranging from open paths to ancient holloways and always in sight of Colmer's Hill, a distinctive high point topped by a group of trees. The ride starts and ends at the excellent Symondsbury Kitchen who can also provide a map. If you are up to it, there is also a more technical (paid for) trail on offer.

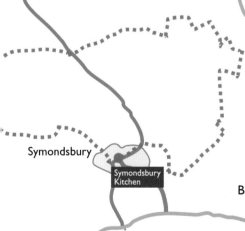

Symondsbury

Symondsbury Kitchen

Bridport

Distance: 6 miles
OS Explorer 116

Ringstead Clifftops

This on/off-road ride begins and ends in the free National Trust car park above Ringstead rather than the lower seaside car park.

The views stretch as far as Portland, silhouetted in the distance and along the switchback chalk coastline of the Purbecks.

The route is easy to follow and the gradients are mostly gentle. There are a few short on-road stretches.

Take care especially on the short busy stretch of the A353.

Distance: 15mls
OS Explorer OL15

Sculpture next to the bridleway

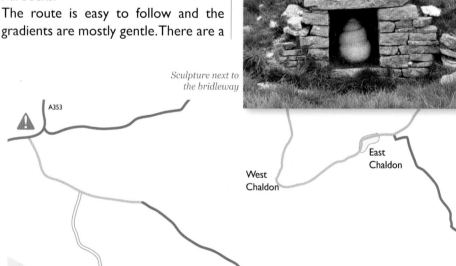

A353

West Chaldon

East Chaldon

Ringstead Bay

This trip takes you along the water's edge from Poole by cycle-path and then along part of Bournemouth's magnificent six-mile-long esplanade as far as its pier.

The round trip is about 12 level miles and a visual feast. The Esplanade is open to bikes except in July and August.

The ride begins at Poole Quay, with the silhouette of Brownsea Island shimmering in the distance. It follows the water's edge to Sandbanks, a popular spot for windsurfers. A cycle lane then takes you through the traffic to the start of Bournemouth Esplanade. On a fine day you could imagine yourself on a Californian boardwalk as roller bladers and joggers fly past.

If you wish, you can combine this trip

Kitesurfing in Poole Harbour

with a visit to the excellent Russell-Cotes Museum and Gallery just a five minute walk from the pier.

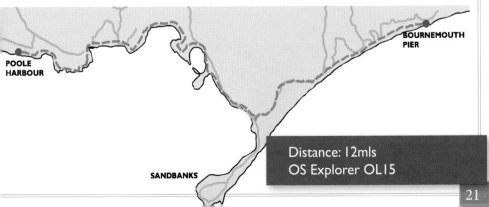

BOURNEMOUTH
PIER

POOLE
HARBOUR

SANDBANKS

Distance: 12mls
OS Explorer OL15

The Blackmore Vale

This is a gentle on-road route where you'll hardly see a car.

After a climb out of Evershot, the route wends its way across gentle downland beneath the chalk escarpments of the Dorset Downs.

Note: It is advisable to dismount and cross the busy A37 on foot!

Worth a detour is St Mary's Church in Melbury Bubb, which possesses an intriguing and exotic font made from the inverted base of a Saxon cross. The sinuous carvings covering it show a definite Norse influence.

The village of Leigh has the scant remains of an ancient miz maze or turf maze and further on you pass the Friary of St Francis a beautifully situated farm open to the public for retreats.

Inverted Saxon font, Melbury Bubb

Distance: 17mls approx
OS Explorer 117

CYCLE

Start at the lay-by below the Hardy Monument. The first part of the ride, a lofty chalk ridge, is lined with the barrows of our Iron Age forebears, who picked a pretty neat spot with sweeping views over Weymouth Bay.

Reaching the road, a right turn onto tarmac carries you on an exhilarating run downhill to the outskirts of Upwey, famed for its wishing well. Eventually a bridleway leads you through open fields, which in spring are alive with the sound of lambs. The path then passes an abandoned farmhouse with the Hardy Monument on the horizon. A gentle uphill cycle brings you back once again to the lay-by.

The route also makes an enjoyable walk.

Distance: 8 miles
OS Explorer OL15

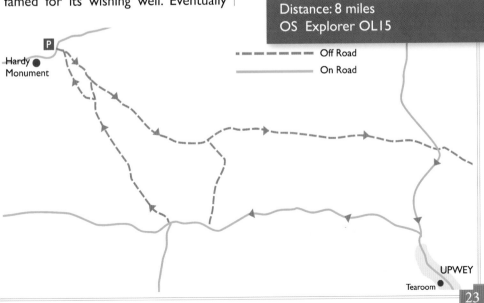

CYCLE

Knowlton, early morning

Starting from Sixpenny Handley this on/off-road route crosses the open downland and big skies of Cranborne Chase. The highlight is the ruined 12thC church of Knowlton. It served a now-vanished hamlet abandoned in the 17thC. What makes it unique is its siting, at the centre of a Neolithic Henge, an unexplained pairing of old and new religions.

Distance: 16 miles
Map: OS Explorer 118

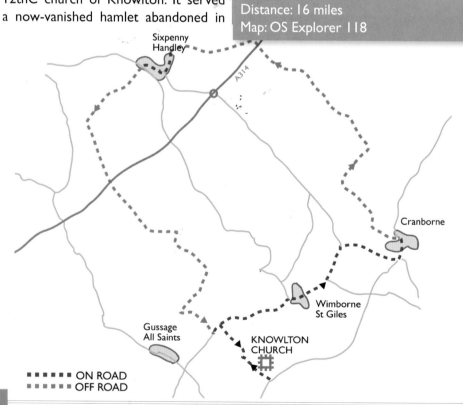

Sixpenny
Handley

A314

Cranborne

Wimborne
St Giles

Gussage
All Saints

KNOWLTON
CHURCH

▪▪▪▪▪▪ ON ROAD
▪▪▪▪▪▪ OFF ROAD

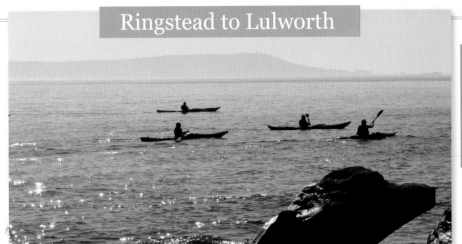

This trip lets you view the Purbecks from a completely new perspective. Ringstead Bay is reached by a long narrow track and except for the essential tea room is quiet and uncommercialised.

You leave Ringstead with the silhouette of the Isle of Portland ever-present on the horizon. Nearing the end of the bay, the terrain rises steeply above you, creating the turf covered cliffs of White Nothe. From here on the dazzling chalk cliffs undulate away into the distance as far as the eye can see. Beneath them, deserted beaches provide perfect picnic spots.

After passing the much photographed natural rock arch of Durdle Door, you soon reach the narrow entrance of Lulworth Cove.

In contrast to Ringstead, Lulworth is a tourist honey-pot but it's impressive all the same.

This is a reasonably long trip and though you can land quite easily, there is no way up the cliffs until Durdle Door.

Take sensible precautions- make sure you are equipped with buoyancy aids, water and have checked the forecast.

Allow a minimum of 4hrs
OS Explorer OL15

RINGSTEAD

LULWORTH COVE
Durdle Door

Poole harbour is one of the largest natural harbours to be found in Europe. It extends for 14 square miles and is dotted with islands, the largest of which, Brownsea Island, is owned by the National Trust. With this amount of safe, enclosed water the harbour just begs to be explored by kayak.

The best place to launch is from a hidden slipway at the end of a suburban road in Hamworthy. To find it, turn off the A35 and follow the signposts for Hamworthy. Soon after passing under a railway bridge, look out for a right turn with what used to be a garage on the corner. Follow this road under a narrow bridge, passing a tall chimney.

The road ends at the slipway. There are no facilities here so bring your own provisions.

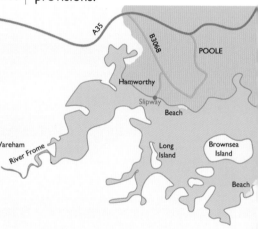

Paddling to the right will take you towards the River Frome where you can paddle as far as Wareham. Paddling to the left takes you towards Sandbanks and Brownsea Island. *Avoid the harbour mouth - the currents can be <u>very</u> strong.*

Take sensible precautions: make su you are equipped with buoyancy ai water and have checked the forecast

The massive expanse of Portland Harbour was built with the sweat of Victorian convict labour. Until quite recently it was an important Naval dockyard. Nowadays the warships are gone and it has become an aquatic playground for yachts, dinghies and windsurfers.

Launching your kayak from the relatively overlooked Castle Cove, around 45 minutes of paddling takes you across the harbour to a sandy landing point beneath Portland Castle one of Henry VIII's defensive forts and open to the public. Walking to the right along the shore brings you to the Harbour Lights bistro, site of the 2012 sailing Olympics, where you can sit taking in distant views of the Purbecks while sipping a latte before returning across the harbour.

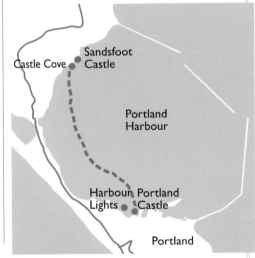

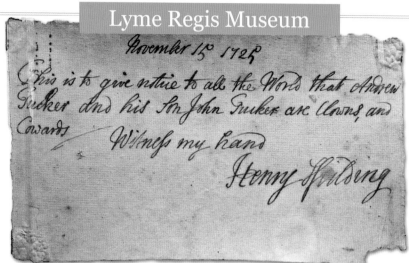

November 15 1725

This is to give notice to all the World that Andrew Tucker and his Son John Tucker are Clowns and Cowards —— Witness my hand

Henry Fielding

Lyme Regis Museum is worth exploring for its quaint stairways and galleries as well as for all aspects of the town's history.

At the top of this page is a hastily written note, dated 1725, written by a young Henry Fielding, author of *Tom Jones*. During a visit to Lyme Regis he fell head-over-heels in love with Sarah Andrews, a local heiress. There were only two problems– she was just 15 and she was already spoken for.

This did not deter Fielding who, aided by his valet, attempted to abduct her on the way to church. Unfortunately, Sarah's local beau, John Tucker and his family thwarted the attempt, but not before punches had been thrown and charges brought.

Fielding left Lyme in a huff soon after, bloodied but not bowed, leaving the following note as his final parting shot.

It reads...*'This is to give notice that Andrew Tucker and his son John Tucker are clowns and cowards*

Witness my hand

Henry Fielding'

Below is the table top made in the 1830s for pioneering geologist William Buckland. What makes it special is that the ornate inlay is not all it first appears. It is made of coprolites, or beetle stones, so called for their beetle-shaped centres. Coprolites have reached us after first taking a rather interesting journey—from the front of a dinosaur and out of the back. In other words it is a tabletop made entirely from dino doos. Buckland was obsessed by it, as the table bears witness.

William Buckland's coprolite table

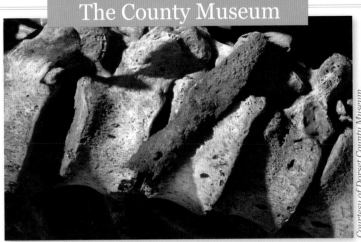

Courtesy of Dorset County Museum.

The County Museum is a purpose-built Victorian building in the centre of Dorchester and tells the story of Dorset from the Stone Age all the way to author Thomas Hardy.

At the top of this page is a detail of the skeleton of one of the Iron Age defenders of nearby Maiden Castle, who was struck in the vertebrae by a bolt from a Roman ballista (a powerful floor standing crossbow) that would have killed him instantly and which still remains where it lodged.

Hardy invented the composting toilet. Moule disagreed with the flushing water closet feeling it caused pollution. With this system, earth mixed with waste produced a usable compost in just a few weeks. Earth from the hopper at the back drops neatly on to the waste at the pull of a lever.

The patented design was exported far and wide across the Empire.

Courtesy Jo Dorset County Museum.

Should an 18thC hangman decide his victim too light for the rope to do its job, he'd attach lead weights to the victims legs. They were called mercy weights for obvious reasons.

In 1852 Rev Henry Moule local philanthopist and a friend of Thomas

Poole Museum stands in the old town close to the quay and was fully refurbished in 2007. A modern atrium leads through to galleries housed in one of the quay's old warehouses.

Wide-ranging displays document the archaeological, social and maritime history of the area.

Poole Harbour has attracted people to its shores since time immemorial. The Romans used it and several of their roads converge on it.

Three hundred years before their arrival, Iron Age sailors were busily constructing the largest primitive boat to be found in Britain.

Above is the result of their labours. It's actually far more impressive than the shot indicates, being amost 10 metres in length, carved from a single oak, with room for 18 people.

It took 40 years to find a way of satisfactorily preserving it. The answer when found was quite mundane, to submerge it in a solution of sugar.

Russell-Cotes Gallery

The Russell-Cotes Gallery is a charming oddity standing on the low cliffs above the beaches of Bournemouth. It is a rare example of a well-preserved Victorian seaside villa that contains a world-class collection of Victorian paintings by such celebrated names as Dante Gabriel Rossetti, the Pre-Raphaelite artist, and Edward Landseer.

The collection forms a neat anthology of some of the best of Victorian and Edwardian art and was assembled by socialites Merton and Annie Russell-Cotes. It is housed in the opulent villa Merton built as a present for his wife.

The building is an exceptional monument to late Victorian taste and for that reason alone is worth the visit.

Rossetti, one of the celebrated artists found in the gallery collection

As Merton Russell-Cotes said,...'I made up my mind to construct it architecturally to combine the Renaissance with Italian and old Scottish baronial styles'

The Russell-Cotes were also avid globe-trotters and souvenirs of their jaunts to Australasia, America, India, the Near East, Africa and the Pacific Islands are on display in the museum.

MUSEUMS

On seeing the staggering collection of tanks at Bovington, the world's largest tank museum, it is easy to overlook the smaller exhibits which tell an equally evocative story.

In 1916 the first tanks

Use of eyes for luck a modern use of an ancient superstion

appeared on the Somme and militarised warfare entered a new dimension. The museum's fine collection of tanks includes some one-of-a-kind models. War, though, remained barbaric and crude despite new technological advances. Inside these lumbering monsters a three man crew shared their claustrophobic conditions with a huge engine in a maelstrom of noise and fumes. In fact half of all deaths in tanks in WWI were caused by carbon monoxide poisoning.

The item at the top of the page, looks more medieval than 20thC, and was a mask issued to tank crews as protection from razor-sharp metal splinters that would slice through confined space when the tank suffered a hit.

Needless to say, the Tommys generally preferred to take their chances than to actually wear them.

Great War helmet that tells its own story

One of the attractions of local museums is that the lack of sophisticated presentation gives them a personal charm that well-funded urban museums often lack.

Portland Museum is a fine example. Occupying a former quarry-worker's cottage, it is filled with objects tracing Portland's timeless relationship with both sea, stone and convicts.

Thrown in for good measure are the intriguing remains of the withered feline mummy shown above. It dates from the 18thC when it was walled up alive in a new house to bring luck and to ward off evil spirits. Portland having been a virtual island until the 1820s meant that superstitions such as this remained potent for far longer that on the mainland of Dorset

Below is a set of convict fetters from Portland prison. It was founded in the 1840s to provide labour to build the Portland breakwaters. Within 20 years it had become a byword for brutality with on average one death a week.

Meanwhile, Victorian tourists would travel from London for a grandstand view of the unfortunate convicts from rooms overlooking the prison yard while quaffing tea and cakes.

There was a time when this instrument, called for obvious reasons a serpent, was a mainstay of the village church orchestra.

The serpent, as well as the orchestras, were swept away with the arrival of new-fangled harmoniums and organs introduced by the Victorians. By Thomas Hardy's time, they had already become the stuff of nostalgia as this quote from 'Under the Greenwood Tree' testifies...

'Times have changed from the times they used to be,' said Mail, regarding nobody can tell what interesting old panoramas with an inward eye, and letting his outward glance rest on the ground, because it was as convenient a position as any, 'People don't care much about us now! I've been thinking we must be almost the last left in the county of the old string players. Barrel-organs, and the things next door to 'em that you blow wi' your foot, have come in terribly of late years.'

'Ay!' said Bowman, shaking his head; and old William, on seeing him, did the same thing.

'More's the pity,' replied another. 'Time was - long and merry ago now! - when not one of the varmits was to be heard of; but it served some of the quires right. They should have stuck to strings as we did, and kept out clarinets, and done away with serpents... 'Yet there's worse things than serpents,' said Mr Penny. 'Old things pass away, 'tis true; but a serpent was a good old note: a deep rich note was the serpent.'

Drawing of the The Church band Sutton Montis 182

MUSEUMS

The Abbey Museum stands next to the site of Shaftesbury Abbey, once home to Britain's leading Benedictine community for women. Though small, it contains an interesting set of finds whilst outside is a garden planted with medieval medicinal herbs.

The above exhibit, looking somewhat like a water-damaged shoebox, tells a fascinating story. It is the humble lead casket that once held the remains of an English king and for centuries was the focus for pilgrimage of the long-gone Abbey of Shaftesbury.

The king was Edward the Martyr, son of the Saxon king, Edgar.

Crowned at just sixteen, Edward was murdered soon after the coronation at Corfe Castle and his remains interred at Shaftesbury around 979 AD.

Edward was canonised in 1001AD and his feast day became one of national veneration and pilgrimage.

Miraculously, centuries after his death Edward's lungs, kept in a glass jar, were reportedly still breathing...

Similar to the recent discovery of Richard III's burial place, the site of Edward's burial was lost for centuries and only discovered during an archaeological investigation on the site of the Abbey in 1933.

While the box still remains above ground, Edward's bones were eventually reburied in a cemetery in...Woking—but that's another story...

Gargoyle from the abbey ruins

The Military Museum occupies a grim looking keep that was originally the entrance to Dorchester's Victorian barracks.

As well as chronicling the Dorset

Tiger's claw

regiment, it is also home to, among other things, Hitler's writing desk salvaged from the ruins of Berlin.

The apparently insignificant objects above became a catalyst for an event that shook the British Empire.

Pre-packed cartridges were introduced in the 1850s as standard issue to Indian native troops. The powder being kept dry by a coating of pork or beef fat, which required the troops biting off the ends before loading them. This was highly offensive to the religious sensibilities of both Muslim and Hindu troops. It caused a simmering of discontent that eventually exploded into bloody rebellion, now known as the Indian Mutiny.

On the left is a *'wagnuk'* or *'tigers claw'*. It was used by an Indian sect called Thuggees, who believed in ritualised murder and robbery. It was used to give the impression that their unfortunate victim had been killed by a tiger.

Augustus John

Blue Poole near Wareham

Portrait of Thomas Hardy

It was in 1911 that bohemian painter, Augustus John, first appeared in Dorset driving a gypsy caravan at the head of an entourage of women, children and hangers-on. They were heading for Alderney Manor, a grandly named crenellated pink bungalow in 50 acres of Poole heathland.

John was already renowned as an artistic genius, though the less generous attributed this genius to a bang on the head while at college.

Alderney became a mecca for the most brilliant creative minds of the era, who stayed in brightly painted gypsy caravans set in the lush grounds. Children ran wild through the heath and animals of all shapes and sizes wandered the grounds- there was even a token monkey.

The chaos was presided over by his wife Dorelia, dressed in flowing Pre-Raphaelite robes.

He was also a notorious womaniser: even Ian Fleming's mother was counted as a mistress. It became almost de rigeur to claim motherhood of one of his many children. Some put the number at a hundred though a more modest nine were acknowledged.

It was said that he patted every child on the head when walking down the Kings Road in case one might be his own.

He meanwhile produced a series of brilliant portraits including those of a couple of the local lights: T. E. Lawrence and Thomas Hardy. Nothing is forever, though, and in 1927 the group upped and moved across the border to Fordingbridge in Hampshire.

Alderney Manor, alas, is now long gone, as is Augustus John who passed away in 1961.

JamesWhistler

Little Rose of Lyme

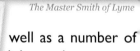

Whistler

The Master Smith of Lyme

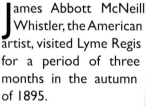

James Abbott McNeill Whistler, the American artist, visited Lyme Regis for a period of three months in the autumn of 1895.

During that time he produced a number of fine portraits as well as a number of lithographs.

The Little Rose of Lyme depicts Rosie Randall, the mayor's daughter, while the subject of the other portrait is *The Master Smith of Lyme Regis.*

View over the Purbecks towards Portland-little changed today

J ohn Constable first visited Dorset in 1816 as the the guest of his close friend Reverend Fisher (later Bishop of Salisbury) who officiated at his marriage.

Osmington

Fisher then invited the newlyweds to honeymoon at his vicarage in Osmington Mills.

Wrote Fisher: *"...My house commands a singularly beautiful view, and you may study from your very window. You shall have a plate set by the side of your easel, without your sitting down to dinner. We* *never see company, and I have brushes paints and canvas in abundance. Of an evening, we sit over our autumnal fireside, read a sensible book, perhaps a sermon, and after prayers, get us to bed..."*

The couple spent six memorable weeks there with Constable producing many sketches some of which he went on to finish in oils.

In 1820 and 1823 Constable again visited Dorset as the guest of Fisher, who was now vicar of Gillingham. Here he painted his celebrated view of Gillingham Mill.

The Mill at Gillingham

ARTISTS

Weymouth Bay

A surprising number of celebrated artists have visited Dorset over the centuries, including J.M.W. Turner. He was a prolific painter and made many painting tours throughout Britain and the Continent. He travelled almost every year and in 1811 toured the Southwest producing a series of paintings which in turn were reproduced as a book of engravings entitled *Picturesque Views of the Southern Coast of England*.

While in Dorset, he painted many of the landmarks that are still recognisable today; including Corfe Castle, Lulworth Cove, Poole Harbour, Lyme Regis and Weymouth.

View of Lyme Bay

View towards Corfe

The creator of English literature's most memorable monster can be found just behind the Bournemouth branch of T K Maxx, in the churchyard of St Peter's.

Mary Shelley, author of *Frankenstein* was one of the 19thC's rebels. The daughter of the radical thinker, William Godwin, she became profoundly influenced by the intellectuals she met. In 1814, aged 17, she fell in love with one of them, an impoverished poet named Percy Bysshe Shelley with whom she eloped to France leaving behind his pregnant wife. To add to the scandal they were accompanied by Mary's half sister.

Mary now found she was pregnant, though the unfortunate suicide of Shelley's wife left the couple free to marry. Her baby, a girl, lived just a few months. Within a short time Mary was pregnant again and once more the three of them accompanied by her new baby boy set off across Europe arriving in Geneva to spent the summer with Lord Byron. Bad weather meant the party passed the time telling and writing ghost stories. All are now forgotten except Mary's *Frankenstein,* now a timeless classic. With Shelley's encouragement she published the novel in 1818 as *Frankenstein, or The Modern Prometheus.* It was an immediate success. She was just 21.

Then tragedy. struck. Shelley drowned when his yacht was wrecked in a storm off the Italian coast. His remains were cremated on the beach where they were found. The idyll had ended.

Mary returned to England to eke out the rest of her life as a writer, dying at 53 years. Her son buried her near his home in Bournemouth, where she now lies forgotten under a drab Victorian slab yards from the main street.

In a final macabre twist, on her death Mary's writing box was found to contain Percy Shelley's heart, wrapped in a sheet of paper, on it was written his poem *Adonais*. It now lies beside her in the her grave.

J. Mead Faulkner

Moonfleet is a classic tale which has been adapted many times for television and radio. The original book though, deserves to be read. Whatever your age you won't be disappointed.

The author, J. Mead Faulkner, wrote just three books. He was a successful businessman and became the Chairman of Armstrong Whitworth Co., one of Britain's major armaments manufacturers; a post he held throughout the crucial years of the First World War. He also reached physically dizzying heights, measuring an amazing 6-foot 9-inches in his socks.

His novel, *Moonfleet* is based upon memories of his childhood in the Purbecks and weaves a colourful yarn of smugglers and smuggling.

The story takes its inspiration from the small hamlet of Fleet, near Abbotsbury, that stands close to the large expanse of brackish water behind the Chesil Bank also called The Fleet. The village was almost entirely destroyed in 1824, when a terrible storm breached Chesil Bank washing away much of the village, drowning 28 people and leaving just the church standing.

Fleet Church

Benjamin Jesty

Until the 18thC smallpox was a scourge.

Those lucky enough to survive it would have their looks destroyed by the disfiguring pockmarks it left. Queen Elizabeth was a celebrity survivor who resorted to covering the resulting scars in thick white make-up.

The disease had no cure until a Dorset farmer, Benjamin Jesty of Yetminster, noticed that milkmaids, infected with cowpox, a milder form of the disease, consequently developed an immunity to smallpox. In 1774 he used his family as guinea pigs, infecting them with cowpox. Scatching their skin with a darning needle he transferred the cowpox matter to the scratch. The experiment proved a success with his sons becoming immune to smallpox.

His discovery, though, went largely unrecorded and while he carried on with innoculations locally others stepped forward to claim credit. It was not until 1806 he finally received the accolade he deserved.

The portrait above was painted at the time he presented his case in London to the Original Vaccine Pock Institute. An unassuming farmer, he refused to dress for the occasion, preferring his normal everyday country clothes.

He died in 1816 and lies buried at Worth Matravers.

Contemporary print satirising the effects of smallpox innoculation

43

*Emperor Vespasian
conqueror of Dorset*

Rome's conquest of Dorset and the Southwest was led by future emperor, Vespasian, who would later be responsible for the brutal sack of Jerusalem.

The locals stood little chance against the onslaught of his well organised legions. Evidence of battle, slingstones and mass graves were discovered at Maiden Castle on the outskirts of Dorchester in the 1940s.

Dorchester itself was originally the Roman town of *Durnovaria* and has proved rich in artefacts, many of which can be found in the County Museum.

The remains of their long occupation, though, are surprisingly scant. Here are the best examples.

TOWN HOUSE *Dorchester*

This site is the best preserved example of a Roman town house in the country.

Excavations in 1937 revealed a complex of eight buildings dating from the early 4thC AD. It was adorned with costly mosaics and painted plaster around 350AD. The Roman Town House can be seen in the grounds of County Hall, Dorchester.

ROMAN ROAD *Puddletown Forest*

Only recently rediscovered, it was originally part of a road that ran from Exeter to London. Remains run for half a mile and take the form of a bank more than 15ft high with ditches either side.

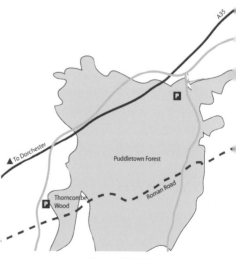

Course of the Roman road

Mosaic, Town House, Dorchester

ROMAN AQUEDUCT *Dorchester*

The aqueduct ran for about 12 miles from Notton to Dorchester and places where it was cut into the hillside can still be seen. Originally it was about 5 feet wide and 3 feet deep and delivering eight million gallons a day to the town.

ACKLING DYKE ROMAN ROAD

The route of the road runs arrow-straight for 22 miles from the outskirts of Salisbury to the hill fort of Badbury Rings cutting through any pre Roman monuments which happened to be in its way. The road can be easily followed as it is a right of way. Much of the road takes the form of a raised bank or 'agger' for drainage.

ROMAN TEMPLE *Maiden Castle*

It was constructed about 400AD similar in plan to that at Jordan Hill, near Weymouth. It is beautifully situated within the ramparts of the hillfort of Maiden Castle, looking across the fields to Roman Dorchester.

MAUMBURY RINGS *Dorchester*

Originally a Neolithic henge, this large circular earthwork in the centre of Dorchester is 85 metres in diameter. It

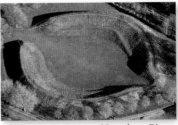
Maumbury Rings

was adapted by the Romans to serve as a amphitheatre and in the 17thC as a place of execution.

ROMAN TEMPLE *Weymouth*

Only the foundations are visible of this 4-5thC square columned temple. Various ritual foundation deposits were discovered as well as the remains of about a 100 burials in the area surrounding it. The atmospheric site is situated at Jordan Hill with fine views of Weymouth Bay.

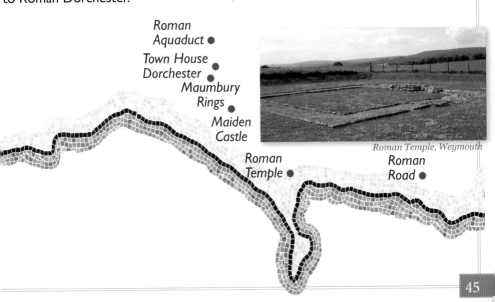

Roman
Aquaduct ●
Town House
Dorchester ●
Maumbury
Rings ●
Maiden
Castle

Roman
Temple ●

Roman Temple, Weymouth

Roman
Road ●

The Lost Mansion

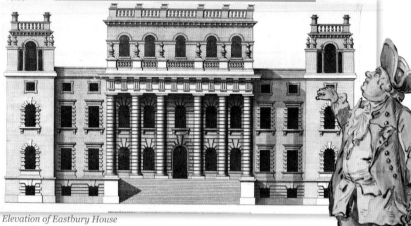

Elevation of Eastbury House

If you need a lesson in pointless vanity, you need look no further than Tarrant Gunville in North Dorset.

Close to the village stands a monumental gateway that leads into a private park. This once formed the grand entrance to Eastbury House built for George Bubb Doddington.

Of humble origins, Doddington's life was transformed after inheriting an enormous fortune. He used it to become a force in Georgian politics and a confidante of both George III and the Prince of Wales.

Like most social climbers, he had an insatiable desire to impress, and Eastbury House was to be the ultimate expression of this. Completed in 1738, it took two decades to build at a cost of around £8,000,000 in present day terms. By then it was one of the grandest stately homes in the country and only slightly smaller than Blenheim Palace, which shared the same architect.

Bubb Doddington was portrayed as fat and dissipated, despised by his fellow politicians. But he was keen to surround himself with the trappings of culture: Voltaire and Fielding were both guests at Eastbury at one time or another.

Contemporary sketch of George Bubb Doddington

On his death in 1762, the house became a massive white elephant and a year later, just 24 years after completion, Eastbury House was levelled to the ground. With the exception of part of the kitchen wing and a pair of monumental gateposts, nothing now remains.

As Eastbury House would have looked- Blenheim Palace

Blandford Forum is one of the few towns in Dorset where you can bellow out an expletive and not raise eyebrows. You may even receive a pat on the back...

The reason for this can be traced to a warm summer's day in 1731.

In a scenario reminiscent of the Great Fire of London, sparks from a local soap boiler's ignited thatched roofs. Flames, fanned by a fresh breeze, were soon licking out of control. Within 24 hours much of the town including its church had been reduced to ashes.

The biggest losers in the conflagration and its greatest benefactors were two local entrepreneurs, Thomas and Richard, who possessed the interesting surname of Bastard. They were to devote the next 30 years directing and partially financing an enlightened restoration of the town. The higgledy piggledy street plan was swept away, and under their auspices replaced with today's fine Georgian town.

Indeed Blandford Forum is now one of the most elegant and complete Georgian towns in Britain.

Long live those Bastards!

Recipe for regeneration take one careless tallow chandler and two ingenious Bastards

Modern inscription in the pavement in Blandford

Contemporary fire engine in Goldhill Museum, Shaftesbury

T.E Lawrence

T.E. Lawrence was one of the great heroes of the 20th century. During World War I he masterminded a revolt of the Arabs against their Turkish rulers. The film *Lawrence of Arabia* is based on that momentous phase of his life.

After the war, Lawrence was feted as a hero but, disillusioned with postwar politics, he sought anonymity and joined the Tank Corps as a private at Bovington Camp in Dorset under a pseudonym. While there, he rented and finally bought a spartan, isolated cottage near Wareham, Clouds Hill, selling his gold dagger from Mecca to pay for its renovations. Here he found the peace and quiet he needed to work on *Seven Pillars of Wisdom*, his evocative autobiographical account of the Arab Revolt.

Lawrence was killed in a motorcycle accident just a few hundred yards from Clouds Hill in 1935.

His cottage is now a National Trust property, and contains much of his original furniture and possessions.

The T. E. Lawrence display at the Tank Museum includes

©National Trust Images/Dennis Gilbert

Lawrence's hideaway-Clouds Hill

rare film footage and a Brough Superior motorcycle similar to the one he was riding at the time of his fatal accident, while Wareham Town Museum features a whole section on Lawrence with documents relating to his life in Dorset and the Middle East.

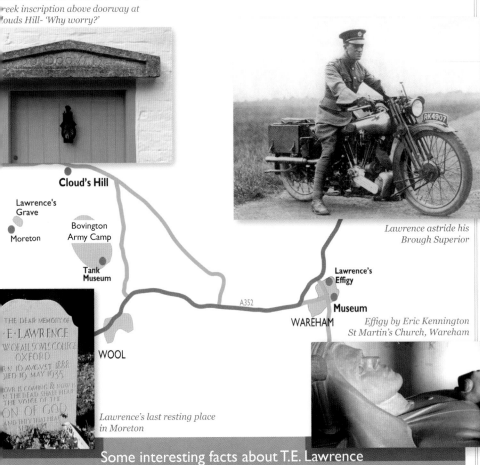

Greek inscription above doorway at Clouds Hill- 'Why worry?'

Lawrence astride his Brough Superior

Cloud's Hill

Lawrence's Grave

Bovington Army Camp

Moreton

Tank Museum

A352

Lawrence's Effigy

Museum

WAREHAM

WOOL

Effigy by Eric Kennington St Martin's Church, Wareham

THE DEAR MEMORY OF
T·E·LAWRENCE
FELLOW OF ALL SOVLS COLLEGE
OXFORD
BORN 16 AVGVST 1888
DIED 19 MAY 1935

Lawrence's last resting place in Moreton

Some interesting facts about T.E. Lawrence

- He was a dedicated vegetarian and neither smoked nor drank.
- He was born out of wedlock to the family governess.
- After the war, he changed his name twice to keep his privacy.
- He was working as an archaeologist at the outbreak of the Great War.
- Lawrence was just 5-ft 4-in tall.

- He lost the original manuscript of *Seven Pillars of Wisdom* in 1919 at Reading station. It was never found.
- *Seven Pillars of Wisdom* has never gone out of print.
- He walked 1,100 miles in three months across mountains and deserts to understand Arab life.

Bridport Rope Industry

It's hard to believe that within recent memory the bustling town of Bridport was the centre of an industry stretching back a thousand years or more–the manufacture of rope.

So synonymous did Bridport become with this product that in the 18thC the hangman's rope, was nicknamed 'The Bridport Dagger'.

The industry was established because the surrounding countryside provided perfect conditions for growing flax and hemp, raw materials for rope making. Records of rope manufacture date back to the 12thC when King John placed large orders for rope and cordage for his navy.

Spinning rope in a ropewalk

Rope making and the production of sail cloth eventually employed more than half of Bridport's population; production methods changed little until the late 19thC.

Manufacture consisted of a number of quaintly named processes;

RETTING Harvested flax was rotted in ponds or the fields to separate the stems from the fibres.

SCALING The hemp was stripped from the stems.

BOLLING The stems were crushed to remove the woody parts. This was where the first mechanisation appeared; water mills were equipped part time with special hammers to pound the flax.

SCUTCHING or SWINGLING This removed the crushed woody part.

HACKLING Lengths of raw fibre were drawn though closely placed metal spikes like wire hairbrushes to make the fibres run in one direction. An arduous job, carried out by men.

SPINNING Turned the fibre into high quality rope, which became renowned throughout Britain: whether providing nets for the distant Newfoundland fisheries or the myriad lines and cables used on the Navy's wooden ships.

The process of spinning also gave Bridport a distinctive layout. Behind the small cottages lining the high street remain long, narrow alleys, now generally converted to gardens. They provided the rope walks where the the rope was 'spun', a process which until the mid-nineteenth century was carried out by hand, usually by women and children.

At one end of the walk stood a simple wooden building called a turnhouse which housed the reel on which the completed twine was wound. This was usually turned by a child (often as young as six) sitting in a pit. Women, gradually fed out hanks of flax or hemp fastened around their waists, the ends attached to the spinning wheel, as they moved backwards away from the turn house. The newly-made rope was supported at intervals by being hooked over upright posts known as skirders. It was a process that was carried out rain or shine, often far into the night when the women would fix a candle to each shoulder to illuminate their labours.

The rope industry also gave rise to net-making. Nets were braided using the twine in a process rather like knitting on a large scale using a braiding needle. As with any industry, demand was fickle. The Navy eventually found it was cheaper to spin its own rope closer to its dockyards; luckily demand was replaced by the growth of the East India Company, while the Newfoundland fisheries (almost entirely fished by Westcountry men) created an ever-growing demand for nets.

Towards the 19thC the rope-making processes were gradually centralised in mills, though it was many years before the use of outworkers was abandoned. During the 20thC the industry became concentrated into of the hands of Gundry's, founded by Jacob Gundry in 1665. Gundry's is now a multi-million pound company, part of a much bigger organisation Marmon Holdings who still market nets from Joseph Gundry's original works.

Skirder

Rope spinner

Buttony,' as Dorset's button making industry was known, originated in Shaftesbury in the 17thC and was once an important cottage industry in East Dorset. There were several distinct styles–the Dorset knob, high tops, bird's eyes as well as the cross wheel (above, from the Blandford Costume Museum). It is very hard to believe that each button, a piece of miniature macrame, was individually hand-woven round a metal ring.

'Winders and dippers' formed the wire rings while 'stringers' wove the actual buttons. Button makers could each turn out a gross a day and their products were exported across the world. They even had royal approval... Charles I went to the block wearing a waistcoat embellished with Dorset Buttons. The industry lasted until the 1850s when the introduction of the button machine caused the industry to disappear almost overnight causing many of the buttoners to emigrate to the New World rather than face starvation.

Francesca Evans

On the outskirts of Lyme Regis stands an elegant Georgian villa, once the home of novelist John Fowles. Two centuries earlier it was the summer residence of Eleanor Coade.

Mrs Eleanor Coade was a rare beast in Georgian England: a female entrepreneur. Born in Lyme in 1733, she moved to London when quite young. In 1769 she bought a struggling artificial stone manufactory on the banks of the Thames. In two years she had transformed the business, perfecting a product that revolutionised the architectural landscape of Georgian England.

Her factory created a revolutionary new material known as Coade Stone that was impervious to the acid pollution created by industry. It was not only resilient but retained fine detail, making it perfect for statuary.

It was baked twice in a kiln rather than hardened with a chemical reaction.

Monumental lion, originally from the Red Lion Brewery, now on Westminster Bridge, London

The new material was eagerly adopted by the finest architects, such as John Nash.

It also embellished both the Royal Pavilion and Buckingham Palace. Examples have also been found as far afield as Russia and the Caribbean, ranging in size from one inch to 16 feet. Belmont, too, is richly decorated with the artificial stone for which Eleanor Coade is famous. After lying empty since John Fowle's death, the house has a bright future. The Landmark Trust has lovingly restored the building and it is now available for short lets.

Contemporary engraving of the Coade Stone manufactory

Strangely, given the popularity of the product, the manufactory closed less than 20 years after Mrs Coade's death. Today the Royal Festival Hall covers the site.

The Easton Massacre

High on Portland sits the church of St George, a classical gem listed in Simon Jenkins' *1000 Best Churches*. Its graveyard is also rather special, being filled with unusually elaborate and evocative memorials, a stone's throw from the very edge of a deep quarry.

St George's standing at the very edge of the quarries

In present times, when atrocities are occurrences that take place far from home, a particular memorial is witness to a series of events that shook Portland more than 200 years ago. Events that ended with the violent death of 21-year-old Mary Way. Her gravestone says she was shot and killed by the press-gang.

The incident took place on April 2nd 1803 and is remembered as the Easton Massacre. The story unfolds on the night before her death when men from the frigate Eagle came ashore and attempted to press Nicholas Way. He was the captain of a small vessel and theoretically exempt from the press-gang, as indeed were all the able-bodied men on Portland.

Undeterred, at 5 the next morning the Eagle's captain returned with a heavily armed force of some 30 men and officers. The hour was chosen to catch the islanders while they slept.

They again apprehended Nicholas Way

as well as Henry Wiggat. By this time, the villagers, who were woken by the furore, ran for cover in panic. As the press-gang chased them uphill, they found their way was

St George's churchyard

bravely blocked by Zachariah White, who demanded the source of their authority. The warrant he was shown, signed by the Mayor of Weymouth, bore no legal authority on Portland. The sailors ignored all protestations and moved on.

As the situation began to turn ugly, the soldiers retreated into a defensive line. An attempt to snatch yet another islander caused the crowd's patience to snap. In the ensuing scuffles, a pistol, whether accidentally or not, was fired by the captain. This was the prearranged signal to open fire. In the chaos three of the islanders died instantly, shot through the head. Two more, one of them Mary Way, fell fatally wounded to the ground, a bullet lodged in her back. The press-gang who had also sustained casualties then retreated taking their hard-won captives.

An official enquiry into the events was eventually held but no convictions were ever made, while the involvement of a Weymouth JP only served to sustain the historical enmity between the two communities.

This short walk takes you to the headstone of Mary Way. Also to be found in the churchyard is the grave of doubly unfortunate William Hansford, who after breaking his leg during the Great Storm of 1824 was killed when his house was toppled by the storm. Park in Chiswell and follow the signs for the coast path, which takes you steeply uphill, giving you breathtaking views of Chesil Bank and the Jurassic Coast. As the path levels out, a diversion to the left will take you into the Tout Quarry Sculpture Park (see p86), where sculptures lie waiting to be discovered amid the undergrowth.

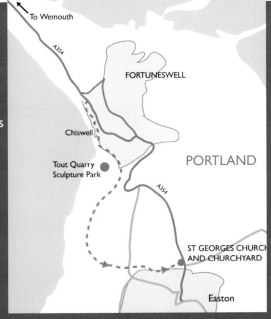

To Wemouth
A354
FORTUNESWELL
Chiswell
Tout Quarry Sculpture Park
PORTLAND
A354
ST GEORGES CHURCH AND CHURCHYARD
Easton

George III by the sea

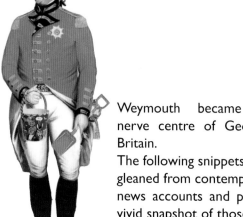

When King George III decided to holiday in Weymouth, its fortunes were transformed overnight. Ministers, socialites and tourists descended on the town. For a few short months each year Weymouth became the nerve centre of Georgian Britain.

The following snippets were gleaned from contemporary news accounts and paint a vivid snapshot of those long lost Georgian summers.

On Friday afternoon at a quarter past five o'clock their Majesties and the six princesses arrived in perfect health at Gloucester Lodge, Weymouth. They set out from Windsor soon after five, breakfasted at Hartford Bridge, partook of a cold collation at the Bishop of Salisbury's at Salisbury Palace and dined at Weymouth.

In the evening the Royal Family walked a considerable time on the Esplanade. A number of boats and pleasure yachts performed several manoeuvres in the bay, which the King seemed mighty pleased with.

During the display of fireworks at Weymouth a servant of Lord Paulet's was unfortunately standing near a hamper of fireworks when they exploded and one of the sticks of rockets entered his groin with such force as to produce mortification, of which he has since died.

On Wednesday morning two privates were shot on Bincombe Down, near Weymouth for desertion. They had stolen a boat from the harbour with intent to go to France, but by mistake landed in Guernsey.

View of Weymouth in 17thC -Gloucester Lodge, the King's residence situated at the centre of the Esplanade still stands

Edward Eastman, a guard of the Royal Weymouth Mail, in coming from Weymouth on Tuesday, fell from the roof and suffocated in the mud. He was not missed by the coachman until the mail reached Basingstoke, four miles from where the unfortunate man fell. He survived about three minutes after being found.

Yesterday Mr Pitt returned to town from Weymouth.

The Royal Family are every day more and more endearing themselves to the people by their habits of familiarity, condescension and manners. The higher orders of subjects well know the amiable qualities of the family; and now the middle and lower orders speak of them with rapture and a glow of heart-felt expression almost bordering on idolatry.

The King has ordered £500 to be distributed among the inhabitants of Weymouth and Portland Island.

Last evening two balloons were exhibited to a number of spectators. The one by night had a fine effect, and as the evening was remarkably calm, it ascended to a remarkable height, till it was lost to the eye below.

17thC print of King George bathing at Weymouth

The Bathing Machines make God Save the King their motto over all their windows, and those bathers that belong to the Royal dippers wear it in bandeaux on their bonnets to go into the sea and have it again in large letters round their waists to encounter the waves...nor is this all. Think of the surprise of His Royal Majesty the first time of his bathing. He had no sooner popped his royal head under water than a band of music, concealed in a neighbouring machine struck up God save great George our King.

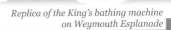

Replica of the King's bathing machine on Weymouth Esplanade

Wreck of the Halsewell

Over the centuries the Purbecks have been the graveyard for innumerable sailing ships.

The Halsewell, returning from Madras in 1784 is just one example. Its fate not only aroused the sympathy of the nation, but inspired a painting by J.M.W. Turner.

Beside her crew, the ship was carrying a number of passengers, including the captain's daughters. Fatefully this was Captain Pearce's final voyage before he

took retirement.

On encountering a tremendous storm in the Channel, the vessel was finally driven against the cliffs at Seacombe near Worth Matravers. The ship was then washed broadside against a natural cave in the cliff face allowing many of the unfortunates to scramble to apparent safety. The cliff above, though, proved almost impossible to climb in such atrocious conditions. Just two sailors made it to the top to alert the local villagers, while those left behind gradually succumbed to cold and exhaustion. More than 80 people were eventually rescued but 160 perished in the freezing waters, including the captain who chose death rather than to abandon his two young daughters.

The ship, meanwhile, sank without a trace while the bodies recovered are reputed to lie buried in mass graves on the cliff tops.

George III, holidaying in nearby Weymouth, visited the spot to pay his respects and gave a reward of £100 in appreciation of the efforts of the local villagers.

The site has since proved a small treasure trove of artefacts from the ship's cargo. Everything from a pair of cufflinks depicting an early balloon flight to the ship's hourglass.

In this year, 1348, in Melcombe, in the county of Dorset, a little before the feast of St John the Baptist, two ships, one of them from Bristol came alongside.
One of the sailors had brought with him from Gascony the seeds of the terrible pestilence, and through him the men of that town of Melcombe were the first in England to be infected. **Greyfriars Chronicle**

There can't be many outbreaks of deadly disease celebrated with a plaque as is the case in Weymouth.

It was here that The Black Death first entered Britain from the Continent.

In those days the town was a thriving port. Then, in the middle of the 14thC the following ominous paragraph in the Chronicon Angliae heralded the coming catyclism

"...in Dorsetshire, where, as in other counties, it made the country quite void of inhabitants so that there were almost none left alive."

A contemporary described it thus

"...Woe is me of the shilling in the armpit; it is seething, terrible, wherever it may come, a head that gives pain and causes a loud cry, a burden carried under the arms, a painful angry knob, a white lump. It is of the form of an apple, like the head of an

Plague doctor

onion, a small boil that spares no-one. Great is its seething, like a burning cinder, a grievous thing of an ashy colour. It is an ugly eruption that comes with unseemly haste. It is a grievous ornament that breaks out in a rash. The early ornaments of black death."

Within a short time, 45 percent of the population had succumbed. At a loss to find an explanation, the people found scapegoats, most conveniently the Jews, who had suffered terrible persecution. The pestilence, carried by the fleas of the black rat had gradually spread across Europe from China and was so named from appearance of buboes; hard, painful swellings that appeared in the victim's groin, neck and armpits. the appearance of which meant certain death.

Commemorative Plaque, Weymouth

THE 'BLACK DEATH'
ENTERED ENGLAND IN 1348
THROUGH THIS PORT.

IT KILLED 30-50%
OF THE COUNTRY'S
TOTAL POPULATION

Monmouth Rebellion

Monmouth beach, Lyme Regis

The beach that lies beyond the Cobb Harbour in Lyme Regis is wild and windswept, unike the more benign beaches nearer to the town. It makes a fitting location for Britain's last sea-borne invasion.

One dark night in June 1685 a small fleet of ships landed the disenfranchised Protestant Duke of Monmouth, Charles II's illegitimate son and 83 determined followers who had pledged to wrest back the throne from his Catholic uncle King James II. As he stumbled up the rough shingle, Monmouth's spirits were high, having been assured of enthusiastic support in the West Country. Soon he'd gathered an army of 3,000 supporters.

After a few days in Lyme he marched to Taunton and rather optimistically declared himself king. Soon, though, his luck began *Duke of Monmouth* to fail as other planned uprisings failed to materialise.

The turning point came soon after at Sedgemoor, on the Somerset Levels, where he met the Royalist army. The result was the rout and massacre of his ill-equipped and ill-trained forces, so much so, that they gave the rebellion its name—'*The Pitchfork Rebellion*'. Monmouth fled dressed in shepherd's clothes. His disguise fooled no one and he was soon captured.

Retribution came swiftly—hundreds were hung, drawn and quartered, some on this very beach in the infamous 'Bloody Assizes', while Monmouth himself ended up parting with his head on Tower Hill.

The late D of M beheaded on Tower Hill 15 July 1685

Tacky's Rebellion

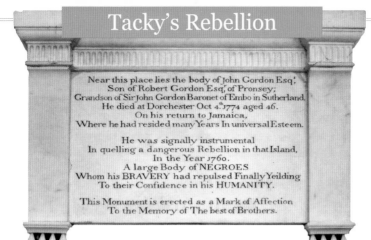

Near this place lies the body of John Gordon Esq.,
Son of Robert Gordon Esq., of Pronsey;
Grandson of Sir John Gordon Baronet of Embo in Sutherland.
He died at Dorchester Oct 4.ᵗʰ 1774 aged 46.
On his return to Jamaica,
Where he had resided many Years In universal Esteem.

He was signally instrumental
In quelling a dangerous Rebellion in that Island,
In the Year 1760.
A large Body of NEGROES
Whom his BRAVERY had repulsed Finally Yeilding
To their Confidence in his HUMANITY.

This Monument is erected as a Mark of Affection
To the Memory of The best of Brothers.

In St Peter's church in Dorchester is an 18thC memorial that commemorates the death in 1774 of John Gordon of the Clan Gordon. It refers to his involvement in the quelling of a slave rebellion in Jamaica in 1760 and the humanity he displayed afterwards.

This uprising, known today as Tacky's Rebellion was one of the first slave uprisings. and its outcome was far from humane as this contemporary account bears witness:

"(...The slaves) marched to another Estate, where the overseer was apprised of their intentions...he opened the door, and wanted to bring them to their duty by speaking to them. Whilst he was doing so, one of his own Negroes shot him in the back. ...They cut off the overseer's head, put his blood in a calabath, mixed gunpowder with it, and eat their plantains dipped in it, as they did by every white man they killed."

Retribution was swift and cruel...

"...There are about 25 of them made prisoner, who are severally carried to Spanish Town and the places they committed their barbarities. Ion who had not been the rebel actually was burnt alive for having sworn to cut his master's and mistress's heads off and make punch bowls of them. ...four more, were found guilty of being concerned in the murder of white people. Two were burnt alive the same day; two were hanged, their bodies burnt, and their heads stuck on poles. Two were tried at Kingston ...Their sentence was to be gibbeted alive 20 feet high. One of them lived nine days without a drop of water..."

There is little evidence of the 'humane treatment' mentioned on the memorial. Tracing John Gordon is now virtually impossible–there were many Gordons present in Jamaica at this time. A John Gordon, though, whose dates correspond with John Gordon of Dorchester, was transported into slavery at nearby Martinique for his involvement in the Battle of Culloden in 1745 so could have well served his time and travelled to Jamaica by 1760 and taken part in this shameful episode, a romantic notion if nothing else!

The pretty North Dorset village of Wimborne St Giles couldn't be further from the bustle of Piccadilly Circus. Both places, though, are forever linked to the Victorian philanthropist Anthony Ashley, Earl of Shaftesbury. The surrounding lands form the ancient seat of the Shaftesburys.

His death in 1893 ended a memorable parliamentary career devoted to fighting the abuse of child labour.

After his burial in Wimborne St Giles, a separate monument in Piccadilly was proposed. Few could have predicted the controversy such a simple idea would cause.

The sculptor chosen, Sir Albert Gilbert Scott, was forced to design not a statue, but a humble fountain. To make matters worse, the London District Council would only supply water to a water fountain with a useful function. Gilbert's eagerly anticipated masterpiece ended up a two level drinking fountain; serving both the public and animals. Things went from bad to worse as the bowl of the completed fountain was too small causing water to drench passers-by.

The fountain was topped by the figure of Anteros, the winged god of selfless love, who stood naked, balanced on one foot loosing an arrow. This was immediately condemned as un-Christian as well as sensual so it was hastily re-branded as the symbol of Christian charity.

Unsurprisingly, Scott refused to attend the opening ceremony. Opinions ranged from ecstatic, *'the finest monument the metropolis possesses,'*... to condemnation... *'indecent or downright dingy'*. There were even calls for the monument to be melted down.

Meanwhile, Scott, facing financial ruin, was forced to flee the country to escape his creditors. When he finally returned, he found that his reviled creation had, for inexplicable reasons, become a national icon, its fame far overshadowing the man it was meant to commemorate.

In a final twist Anteros, perching atop the monument became confused with his brother and opposite, Eros, god of carnal love.

Meanwhile an old wives' tale tells us that Eros is aiming his arrow towards the village green of Wimborne St Giles.

Sir Albert Gilbert Scott   *Earl of Shaftesbury*

The Martyr's Tree

The Martyr's Tree stands on the green in Tolpuddle. In 1834 beneath the boughs of this ancient sycamore, six men, led by George Loveless, forged a simple alliance that would eventually transform British society.

They agreed to join forces to protest against the appalling pay conditions imposed on Dorset farm labourers. Little did they realise that their desperate actions would have such far-reaching consequences.

The landowners used the Unlawful Oaths Act to have them arrested, found guilty and transported to Australia.

They remained unbowed, as Loveless wrote from jail, "We raise the watchword, liberty. We will, we will, we will be free!"

The harsh sentences caused national outrage and they became heroes with 800,000 signatures collected for their release.

The strength of protest meant that by 1837 all six had been pardoned and returned to Britain.

A flame had been kindled which eventually led to the foundation of the Trades Union Movement.

Close by is the Martyrs Museum, which tells the story in full, while every summer the Tolpuddle Festival celebrates these far off events with a weekend of music and marches.

Contemporary images of four of the martyrs: James Brine, Thomas Standfield, John Standfield and George Loveless

The Dorset Quarries

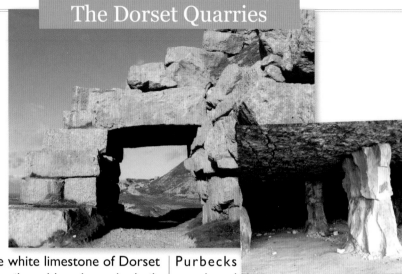

The pure white limestone of Dorset has contributed hugely to the built environment of Britain. Quarrying has been carried out since the Romans. The stone was extracted by cutting into the very face of the cliffs, then simply lowered into waiting ships.

The finest stone was found on Portland and was used notably for Christopher Wren's St Paul's Cathedral, while Purbeck stone tended to be used for more workaday projects. The stone industry in the Purbecks was based to the west of Swanage at quaintly named sites such as Tilly Whim and Dancing Ledge. Workings extended far into the cliffs creating great galleries supported by pillars or 'legs' of stone. The mined stone was then often finished on-site before being lowered by cranes or 'whims' to the waiting ships below.

Nowadays the cliff workings lie abandoned but accessible on foot, starting at Durleston Head and make for exciting exploration, while those on Portland dot much of the coastline.

Swanage

Durles

Tilly Whim
Caves

Seacombe
Cliff

Dancing
Ledge

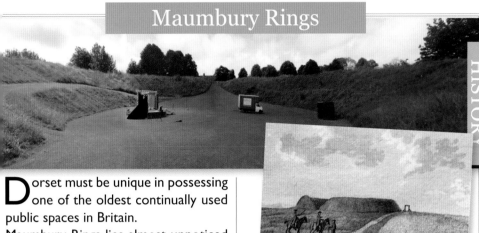

Dorset must be unique in possessing one of the oldest continually used public spaces in Britain.

Maumbury Rings lies almost unnoticed on the busy outskirts of Dorchester, a surprisingly peaceful spot, popular with dog walkers.

It is an ancient earthwork some 85 metres in diameter, erected 2,500 years ago in the Iron Age as a ritual space. Excavations have found it contains 45 mysterious shafts up to 11 metres deep. The arrival of the Romans and the founding of the town of Durnovaria saw the earthwork adapted and remodelled as an amphitheatre.

With the arrival of the Dark Ages, little is known of its use though it must have been an important meeting spot. This was the case in the Middle Ages, when it hosted jousts and revels.

The English Civil War saw a new use, as a Parliamentary fort guarding the road to Weymouth. The gun platform can still be seen in the bank. Around this time hangings and burnings also took place.

18thC print of the rings with the gallows visible on the right

The high banks making an excellent vantage point for the watching crowds.

In fact a story is told of one victim who declined to halt at the inn for a parting glass with the constables.

Listening to his earnest request, they hastened their business, and turned him off just as the postmaster came bearing a delayed reprieve.

Cutting the rope they fetched a surgeon. but he could only shake his head and announce ...'Too late!

...'Sarved him right!' cried the indignant beer swillers standing around, 'he should have stopped for his drink...'

...'Quite the contrary,' retorted the surgeon,...'I will stake my reputation on the fact...the poor fellow has taken <u>a drop too much!'</u>

Nowadays it still holds music events which make use of its excellent acoustics.

The Dorset Clubmen

History records that the English Civil War was an epic struggle between Roundhead and Cavalier. There was, though, a third faction that spontaneously arose consisting of ordinary citizens, who had grown tired of the chaos inflicted on their daily lives. They became known as the Clubmen on account of their simple weaponry. They identified themselves with white ribbons and such slogans as *'If you offer to plunder or take our cattle, be assured we will bid you battle'*

The movement reached Dorset in 1645, and soon their numbers had swollen to 4,000 with a petition drawn up and presented to the warring factions.

Initially, each side thought it prudent to acknowledge the Clubmens' demands until these demands turned to violence. Cromwell and the Parliamentary army finally confronted 2,500 Dorset Clubmen who had occupied the Iron Age hillfort of Hambledon Hill near Child Okeford.

After refusing the Roundheads' peaceful

View from Hambledon Hill

entreaties, they opened fire on the army below. They were no match for the Roundhead cavalry, who quickly gained the summit. The battle became a rout,. Sixty clubmen were killed and hundreds wounded, the rest fled... *'the poor silly creatures'...'sliding and tumbling down that great hill to the hazzard of their necks.'*

With this defeat the movement in Dorset rapidly fizzled out though war continued for six bloody years claiming proportionately more of the population than the Great War.

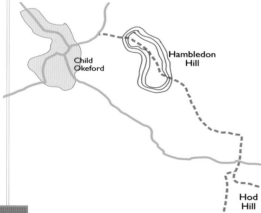

Child Okeford

Hambledon Hill

Hod Hill

The Viking Massacre

During the the building of a new road on the downs above Weymouth several years ago, archaeologists made a unique discovery.

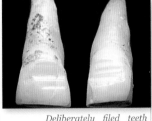

Strewn at the bottom of a pit were the skeletons of around 50 decapitated men, their skulls lying in a neat pile close by.

Skull damaged by ill-aimed sword blow

The site was soon identified as the location of a mass execution dating from the 10thC. DNA tests showed that all of the victims originated from Scandinavia and were aged 18-25, which meant that the victims were very possibly a captured Viking raiding party. If your idea of your average Viking is that of a healthy strapping kind of fellow; the bones show that many definitely weren't. The victims suffered a variety of diseases from gallstones to running sores, while all bore the evidence of savage and inexpert execution.

Adding to the enigma, there were several more skeletons than heads making archaeologists speculate that some heads were taken to be displayed as a warning to others.

Deliberately filed teeth for status or decoration

© Oxford Archaeology

Althouth the actual site has been obliterated by the roadworks, it is possible to view some of the unfortunate victims in a new display at the County Museum in Dorchester.

Jaw sliced through by an inexpert blow

© Oxford Archaeology

The Dorset Pilgrims

The Pilgrim Fathers' first Thanksgiving a celebration a scene repeated ten years later by the Dorset pilgrims

In a Dorchester back street an inconspicuous plaque marks the home of John White, rector of Dorchester between 1606 and 1648.

A staunch Puritan, his influence eventually stretched for many thousands of miles beyond Dorset's county town.

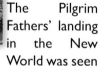

John White's house that stands in the street behind his church

The Pilgrim Fathers' landing in the New World was seen as a God-given opportunity for those persecuted for their faith to worship unmolested. Grasping these possibilities, John White, who was never to make the journey himself, organised the passage of dissenters from Dorset and the Southwest.

Around 10,000 Dorset folk would eventually make this perilous journey which was akin to a 17thC trip to the moon.

Sadly, while the story of the Pilgrim Fathers has passed into history, the story of the plucky Dorset emigrants is overlooked, though the result of their endeavours was the founding of the county town's namesake Dorchester, Massachussets, and, the founding of the state itself.

John White was buried in the porch of St Peter's, though his legacy continued beyond his death, his great-grandchildren John and Charles Wesley, becoming founders of the Methodist Church.

Plaque commemorating the settlers sent by John White in Massachusettes

If you meet a big, hairy bloke shambling down a Dorset lane, he might be just a harmless scrumpy drinker.

However, if you are in the vicinity of Yellowham Woods, near Dorchester and he should lean over, pick up your wife and carry her off, then maybe you've met a *Woodwose*.

The Woodwose is Dorset's very own version of Bigfoot and like his cousin, blurry sightings continue to this day.

The meaning of the first part of his name is obvious while *'wose'* is probably Old English for 'being'. in other words he's a woodbeing.

Woods have always been places of mystery so it's not surprising that legends of hirsute wild men stretch back thousands of years. The Woodwose also had an unfortunate tendency to impregnate the village girls he stole, making him the perfect scapegoat for that night of rural hanky panky.

The legend of wild men appear across Europe. Here on a German coin of 1629

69

The Screaming Skull

Bettiscombe Manor, until recently the seat of the Pinney family, hosts a dark secret.

When John Pinney returned from his West Indian plantations, he was accompanied by a faithful black servant. Soon after arriving the servant fell ill, and from his deathbed he vowed he would not rest until his body was returned to his birthplace. Pinney refused to carry out the dead man's wishes and instead his corpse was laid to rest in the churchyard. Immediately, bloodcurdling screams began to emanate from the dead servant's grave, while the manor house was shaken to its foundations.

After some months the terrified villagers petitioned Pinney to take action. The remains were consequently exhumed and laid to rest in the manor. Now just the the skull remains. Various attempts to remove it from the house have been met with the same unearthly screams. As a result, the skull remains firmly inside the old house.

This is not the end of the story. Local tradition tells of a ghostly carriage rattling between the manor house and churchyard on the anniversary of the servant's death and is referred to as 'the funeral procession of the skull.'

Experts have now reached the conclusion that not only is the skull that of a woman, but it is several thousand years old, probably from a local prehistoric hill fort.

The tale of the screaming skull, though, went on to inspire Victorian novelist Francis Crawford to write a short story the 'Screaming Skull' which in turn led to the making of a 50s Hollywood 'B' movie of the same name.

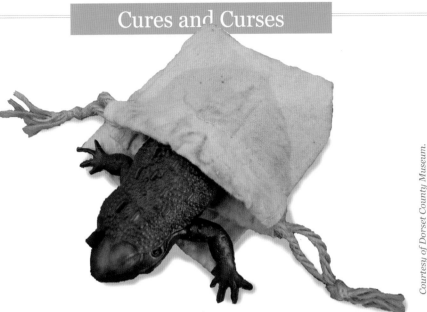

Courtesy of Dorset County Museum.

In the 19thC, James Buckland, self-styled doctor of King's Stag, near Cerne, claimed to cure scrofula with the use of toad bags. An unsuspecting toad's head was pulled off and its still wriggling body put in a bag around the patient's neck. The shock assured a cure. The popularity of this quackery was such that a toad shortage ensued with the result that patients had to make do with toad portions rather than a whole toad.

Each year during a spring full moon Buckland hosted a Toad Fair where his wife and daughter clad in white gowns would hand out his cure to the afflicted.

The practice of sticking pins in wax effigies is well known, though not confined to Dorset. It was referred to by Thomas Hardy in his novel 'The Return of the Native:'

'From her workbasket in the window seat the woman took a paper of pins. These she began to thrust into the image in all directions, with apparently excruciating energy. Probably as many as fifty were thus inserted, some into the head of the wax model, some into the shoulders, some into the trunk, some upwards through the soles of the feet, till the figure was completely permeated with pins.'

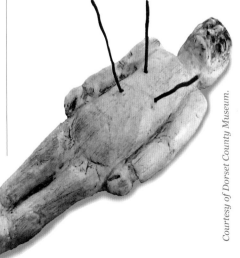

Courtesy of Dorset County Museum.

Dorset's long coastline and ancient seafaring tradition makes it inevitable that tall tales of a fishy variety often circulate amongst the locals.

One of these tell of the sighting in 1757 by the people of Portland of what they took to be a mermaid. The creature, eventually washed up at West Bexington was named Veasta by the locals.

Unfortunately, for local fantasists she was even less of a looker than the local maids, being 13-feet long with a head that was a cross between a man's and a hog's and possessed of a set of 96 pearly teeth. To top things off, she had fins that resembled hands...not the sort of things to have running through your hair.

An even earlier sighting from Portland described a creature resembling a cock appearing from the sea. It possessed a great crest on its head, a red beard and legs half a yard long. After having a good old crow it disappeared from whence it came never to be seen again.

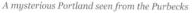

A mysterious Portland seen from the Purbecks

Replica of the Ooser

Streetlights and television have dispelled much of the mystery experienced by our forefathers, yet evidence of ancient dark traditions still exist in Dorset.

One such survival is that of the Dorset Ooser. This took the form of a large grotesque wooden mask with a moveable jaw. The Ooser's function was most likely that of a processional mask, though its true function is lost in the distant past. Way back in the 7thC such masks were already being roundly condemned by the Church.

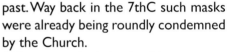

'Whoever at the kalends of January goes about as a stag or bull; that is, making himself into a wild animal and dressing in the skin of a herd animal, and putting on the heads of beast, those who in such wise transform themselves into the appearance of a wild animal, penance for three years because this is devilish.'

This kind of mask was once common throughout the county and theories for Ooser's symbolism vary. Some claim it is a representation of the Devil, while others say it is the representation of a horned deity with its basis in witchcraft or Wicca.

The original Ooser mask disappeared around 1897. A modern copy exists dating from 1975 and makes an appearance each year as part of a procession of Morris dancers who gather at dawn above the Cerne Abbas Giant on May Day and St George's Day.

The original Ooser

Skimmity Riding

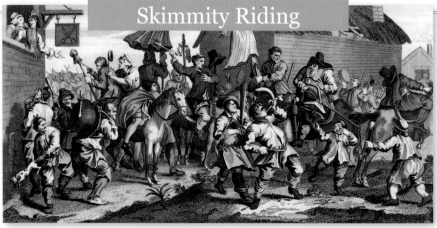

In previous centuries Skimmity Riding was the customary way for neighbours to humiliate perpetrators of marital infidelity.

It took the form of a spontaneous procession in which the victims or their effigies were paraded in a cart or astride a donkey accompanied by the banging of pans and noisy ribaldry.

Though not exclusive to Dorset, it was well documented by novelist Thomas Hardy in *The Mayor of Casterbridge*:

...'They are coming up Corn Street after all! They sit back to back!'

'What–two of 'em—are there two figures?'

'Yes. Two images on a donkey, back to back, their elbows tied to one another's! She's facing the head, and he's facing the tail.'

'Is it meant for anybody in particular?'

'Well–it mid be. The man has got on a blue coat and kerseymere leggings; he has black whiskers, and a reddish face. 'Tis a stuffed figure, with a false face.'

In 1884 the Bridport News reported on one such actual event that occured at Whitchurch Canonicorum–

'About six o'clock in the evening...a strange noise was heard, as of the sound of trays and kettles...three grotesquely attired figures were to be seen escorted by persons dressed in queer and eccentric costumes and who paraded the parish....The figures represented three personages...a male and two females whose past conduct had caused them to be subject to this queer exhibition...one of the females was represented as having an extrordinarily long tongue which was tied to the back of her neck...Those forming the procession were liberally wetted at the various inns...a gallows was erected on which the effigies were hung and afterwards burnt.'

The custom continued into the 20thC with the last recorded incidence of it occuring in 1919.

Portlanders, as they would be the first to admit, have aways felt a race apart. Separated from the mainland by just a narrow causeway and before that, only connected by a ferry, it's understandable that they developed their own distinct character and traditions (see p.95).

One such tradition refers to the mention of the word '*rabbit*' or rather, in this case, <u>not</u> mentioning the word '*rabbit*'.

No one is certain how the taboo first arose but up until very recently was taken very seriously. One explanation surmises that the appearance of fleeing rabbits in large numbers was a sure portent of lethal rockfalls in the quarries for which Portland was famous. Consequently, over time, the cuddly critters became associated with bad luck in general.

As a small aside, Portlanders seem to have been suspicious of everything, even their fellow men.

In a hobbit-like fashion the population arranged themselves into three distinct communities; *Tophillers* (who, obviously lived at the top of the island, *Underhillers* and finally *Kimberlins* (the rest). As for Weymouth folk...well it's best draw a veil at this point.

At first glance this exotic-looking object might seem more at home on the Indian subcontinent rather than in darkest Dorset.

It is called the Byzant and formed the centrepiece of a ceremony of the same name. The Byzant ceremony dates back at least 700 years and took the form of an annual tribute to the Lord of the Manor of Gillingham for the use of his water supplies. Once a year the Mayor and townspeople made their way in a procession with the Byzant at their head to the water source. Here the Lord of the Manor would be presented with the Byzant as well as gifts of gloves, ale, wheaten bread and–vegetarians leave the room–a calf's head. Sadly, the ceremony was discontinued in the 1830s because of, a very modern consideration–the expense!

You can see the Byzant in the Gold Hill Museum, Shaftesbury.

Georgian worthy, John Bastard produced this watercolour (now in Blandford Museum) to mark the passing of an 18thC Blandford landmark, the Damory Oak.

He wrote:

'Damory Oak Supposed to be More than a Thousand years Old. Was in the year 1600 Verry hollow as shown in the plan. And was some time used by 7 people to sell ale there and some times to House Calves, lambs etc. In ye year 1700 it was a verry Hansom Tree and full of Leaves (but hollow as a cove's) Itt sufford in ye ftorm 1703. Since that many good timbers have ben cutt of by ye Rives of Ranston Dorsett. The remainder sold in ye year 1757, as Fier Wood, att 14 pounds sterling.'

At the time it was felled it measured 68 feet in circumference.

Dorset Dialect

William Barnes poet and champion of the Dorset dialect

In 1950 the Society of Dorset Men, on the occasion of their annual dinner, sent a telegram to the king written in the rich dialect of Dorset...

'To *His Majesty King Jarge, Oonce more, the Zociety o' Darset Men, voregather'd round their vestive bwoard at th'Darchester Hotel vor their Yearly Junket, d' zend Yer Most Graishus Majesty their dootiful greetins and expression of unswerven loyalty an' devotion. May Yer Majesty be zpared to us vor many years as our pattern an' guide. I d' bide, vor all time, Yer Vaithful Zarvint and Counsellor...'*

While Northern accents remain strong sadly, the dialect of Dorset seems to be fading, equated as the accent of the plodding yokel. An image problem that now seems too late to rectify.

Here is a small taste of that rich and colourful vocabulary that has all but disappeared...

Axa- *ashes*
A-strout- *stiff stretched.*
Bibber- *to shake with cold*
Blind buck o' Davy-blindman's buff
Bruckly- *brittle*
Chanker- *a wide chink*
Critch- *a big pitcher*
Croodle- *to crow softly*

Dadderdather, dudder- *to amaze or bewilder*
Dumbledore -*a bee*
Emmet- a*n ant*
Gally- *to frighten*
Glutch- *to swallow*
Hidlock- *a hiding place*
Hidybuck- *hide-and-seek*
Slidder- *to slide about*

Randy- *a merry uproar*
Jack-o'-lent- *a man-like scarecrow*
Libbets- *loose-hanging rags*
Nunch- *knob of food*
Pluffy- *plump*
Squot- *to flatten by a blow*
Wops- *wasp*

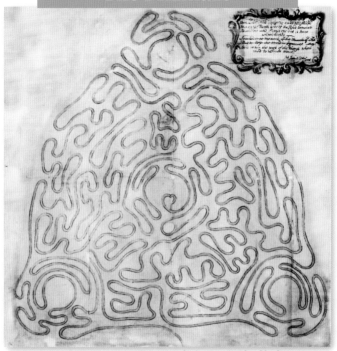

Drawing of Miz Maze in Blandford Museum

John Bastard is generally remembered for his part in the rebuilding of Blandford following its destruction by fire. In his spare time, though, he took a keen interest in his local surroundings. The above drawing is his record of the remains of a Mizmaze or turf maze.

He notes: '*This labyrinth vulgarly called mizmase was on the North side of the road betwixt Blandford and Pimperne but is now Annialated.*'

Supposed to be the work of the Munks of Old But to keep the world in ignorance they said itt was the work of Faierys whom used to dance there'

Mizmazes go back to the dawn of history and are wreathed in legend, though up until the 18thC they were still regularly maintained by villagers. They have all but disappeared from Dorset, though there are some scant remains at Leigh which were recorded as being used as a witches coven. Another maze was to be found at Troytown near Dorchester which took its name from the Old English for a maze—*caertroi.*

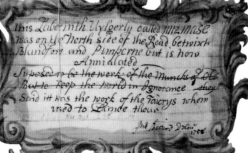

The Jailhouse Cafe

View from Cafe garden

A switchback road climbs higher and higher up the side of the Isle of Portland until finally the forbidding stone gates of the Verne Prison rise up in front of you.

The Victorian prison was established to build the harbour below. Passing through the grim portal, you emerge on to a plateau at the Isle's very highest point, here is journey's end.

The Jailhouse Cafe is an enlightened venture which gives risk-assessed prison inmates a feel for worthwhile work in the community. The food is hearty and staff helpful and friendly. Each seems pumped up to bursting, presumably as a result of hours working out in the prison gym.

On a fine day the views from the lawn, stretch all the way to the Purbecks shimmering in the blue distance. While below massive granite breakwaters girdle Portland harbour: another communal convict effort but of an earlier age.

What on earth would the Victorian lags, breaking the granite for the breakwaters far below, have thought of their present-day counterparts delicately balancing a cappuccino in each hand?

The forbidding Entrance to Portland Prison

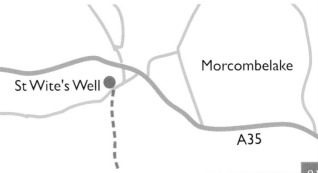

Effigy of St Candida above the church door, Whitchurch Canonicorum

Here is a Dorsetshire hole, but it is no ordinary Dorset hole.

Though unprepossessing, this humble spot is the site of St Wite's Well and has been venerated for centuries.

It can be found in a field close to the busy A35 in Morcombelake and has been considered holy since Medieval times. It was probably associated with the cult of St Candida, whose nearby church was also a place of pilgrimage and veneration.

The clear waters were reputed to cure eye complaints, including blindness while the periwinkles that appear on nearby Stonebarrow every spring, are still known locally as *St. Candida's Eyes*.

St Wite's Well

Morcombelake

A35

The Hidden Chapel

Lying unmarked in the middle of woodlands carpeted with bluebells in the spring, lies the 13thC remains of a Cistercian chapel, now an evocative ruin. It consists of a simple stone arch framing a delicately carved crucifix and stone altar often adorned by simple offerings of flowers left by passing visitors. Within its precincts are three contemporary moss-covered memorial slabs commemorating the deceased owners of this magical spot.

CHAPEL
Chapel Coppice

Abbotsbury Castle

B3157

St Catherine's Chapel

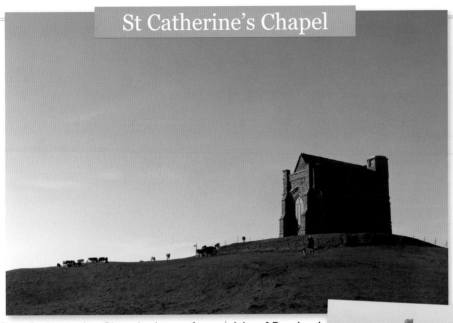

St Catherine's Chapel dates from the 14thC and sits high on a hilltop above the village of Abbotsbury. When built, it served a dual purpose as a place of worship and a landmark for ships, in a similar fashion to the chapel at St Adhelm's Head.

It is a short scramble uphill from the village to gain an outlook that would bring out the poet in anyone. Far below, the Fleet Lagoon sparkles like silver, and Chesil Bank sweeps away in a gentle crescent culminating in the mysterious Isle of Portland. At the foot of the hill are the remains of the abbey that gave Abbotsbury its name.

A short stroll downhill brings you to the endless shingle and the tumbling surf of Chesil Bank itself.

If all this leaves you feeling spiritual, services are still held in the chapel several times a year.

Chesil Beach

The Fossil Forest

If you think this looks like something that might have come from the rear end of a tyrannosaurus, you're reasonably close; this is the best example of a fossil forest on the Jurassic Coastline.

Its spectacular location is a short walk along the coast path on the east side of Lulworth Cove in the Purbecks.

The large stone rings that can be seen were actually formed by algae that surrounded the base of the trees, rather than the trees themselves.

Lulworth
Cove

Fossil
Forest

The Riviera Hotel is a long, low and uncompromising piece of architecture at odds with the surrounding countryside, and is a perfect example of Maritime Deco.

It was built in 1937, rather late for Art Deco, and the outbreak of war meant it was soon requisitioned as a hospital for American troops. When war ended it became first a hotel and then a holiday camp.

Cast concrete and steel don't weather well by the sea and in recent times it had become distinctly tatty. It now has been given a new lease of life by an Arab consortium who have revamped, repaired and generally given the building the kiss of life. The hotel's situation rivals the real Riviera with unhindered views across the sweep of Weymouth Bay.

The main building is a two-storey crescent relieved in the middle by a square central tower. Its facade is a series of arcades that give every room the same magnificent view across the bay. The architect, L. Stewart Smith's deft use of proportion means that though plain, the Riviera is never boring.

Tout Quarry

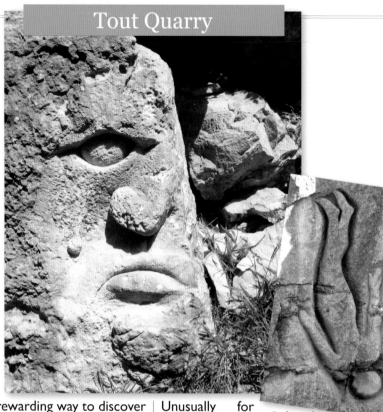

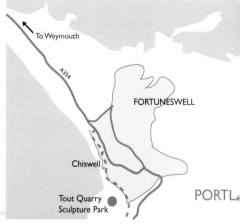

Sculpture by Anthony Gormley

The most rewarding way to discover Tout Quarry, is by taking a short, stiff climb upwards along the coast path from the hamlet of Chiswell. The stunning views alone makes it worth the strain on the heart. The quarry was redundant until 1985 when someone had the elegantly simple idea of turning sculptors loose on the tumbled stone. The result is the best sort of art, the kind you discover almost by lucky accident.

Unusually for contemporary art, it even contains a smattering of wit. Anthony Gormley has made a contribution. There are also sculpture courses that take place within the quarry.

Chesil Bank

To Weymouth

A354

FORTUNESWELL

Chiswell

Tout Quarry
Sculpture Park

PORTL.

A Sylvan Landscape

The notes of a church organ calls schoolboys to Communion in Milton Abbey Church as the early morning sunlight spreads long shadows across the grassy sward stretching to the distant wooded hills. It is the most quintessential of British views.

However, all is not as it seems–this idyll was created at great cost and effort, involving the wholesale removal of a town as well as the sculpting of the valleys and hillsides that converge at this point.

In 1752, Lord Milton, having already rebuilt his manor house in Strawberry Hill Gothic, decided to remodel 500 acres of surrounding countryside in the fashionable pastoral style. To do so he employed Lancelot 'Capability' Brown, the 18thC's most famous landscape designer.

Firstly, the town of Middleton that clustered around the old abbey church was demolished and a lake created. The town's inhabitants were then moved out of sight to the model village of Milton Abbas.

Hedgerows were then swept away and the hilltops heavily forested. As an eyecatcher Lord Milton was lucky to have a medieval pilgrims' chapel on the hill above the manor house up to which a flight of turf steps was laid.

Finally, 16 miles of carriageways were created from which to admire the new views.

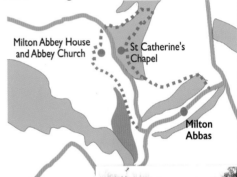

St Catherine's Chapel

Under the auspices of Milton Abbey school this special landscape now remains very much as Lord Milton imagined it. (see p.10)

Hardy Country

Higher Bockhampton

EXPLORE

Thomas Hardy's birthplace, situated at Higher Bockhampton, is a thatched cottage, while his home in latter years, walked many times when visiting his family at Bockhampton.

The route passes through the grounds of Kingston Maurward, a beautiful Palladian pile, now an agricultural college, and then past the Old Manor, an exquisite late Elizabethan mansion.

From Max Gate it's a 20-minute stroll into Dorchester to the County Museum which holds a collection of Hardy memorabilia, including his desk.

Max Gate

Max Gate, is a rather austere Victorian pile designed by Hardy himself. Both are owned by the National Trust and lie close to Dorchester.

Being just a few miles apart it is possible to walk or cycle between the two, along the footpaths and lanes that Hardy must have

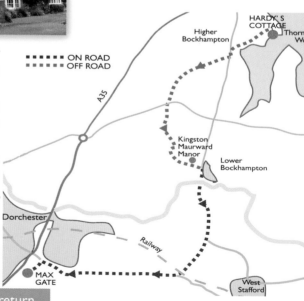

ON ROAD
OFF ROAD

HARDY'S COTTAGE
Higher Bockhampton
Thorne Wo
A35
Kingston Maurward Manor
Lower Bockhampton
Dorchester
Railway
MAX GATE
West Stafford

The Cannington Viaduct

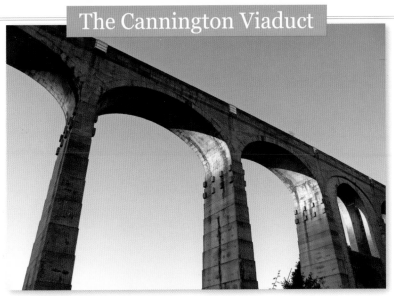

Ancient Rome? No! Railway Modern. The Cannington Viaduct strides across this hidden valley with all the self-confidence of Empire. British, though, rather than Roman. Its monumental arches create a breathtaking focal point in the soft green valley surrounding it.

You don't have to be an enthusiast to admire this spectacular piece of railway architecture. It was constructed in 1902, simply to carry the now defunct Lyme Regis branch line.

The viaduct was ground-breaking too, being one of the first structures to be cast entirely of concrete. Time passed, and like the Roman viaducts before it, so did its raison d'être as the last train rattled over it in 1965. Local folklore tells that it was supposedly sold to a bungee jumping company for 1p, though it never seems to have been used for that purpose.

The best time to see it is early in the morning or in the evening when the golden light of the sun makes it glow.

A rewarding way to reach the viaduct is to follow this 3.75mile walk.
Map: OS Explorer OL15

Church

UPLYME

Cannington
Viaduct

——— Road
- - - - Footpath

EXPLORE

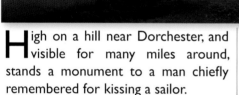

Admiral Thomas Masterman Hardy

High on a hill near Dorchester, and visible for many miles around, stands a monument to a man chiefly remembered for kissing a sailor.

The Hardy Monument is a rather squat, ugly edifice, erected in 1844 to the memory of the other Hardy, Trafalgar veteran, Admiral Thomas Masterman Hardy.

Hardy, was born in 1769 at Long Bredy and lived close by at Portesham.

He was captain of the Victory at Trafalgar when his dying friend, Nelson, uttered those three fateful words, *'Kiss me Hardy,'* so consigning Hardy to be the butt of eternal schoolboy jokes.

There is also another, more prurient version of these events, with Nelson's dying words being interpreted as *'Kismet, Hardy'—meaning—Fate, Hardy.'*

From the top of the monument, you can see over most of Dorset. Footpaths and bridleways radiate away to all points of the compass.

Clavell Tower

High above Kimmeridge Bay stands Clavell Tower, a folly built in 1831 by the Reverend John Richards. In those days people with money were people with style. It stands perilously close to the cliff edge, making the most of the stunning views along the coastline; the tower was so close, in fact, that it was in danger of toppling into the sea. Then a saviour appeared on the scene, The Landmark Trust.

After rebuilding the tower 80 feet further inland, they then set about its complete renovation. The result, unveiled in 2008, is now available for holiday rental.

Portland Bill

The Bill lies at Portland's furthest tip. Here strong currents meet, causing the waters to boil and froth like the contents of a devil's cauldron.

It is therefore surprising to find that the first pair of lighthouses only appeared in 1716. These were replaced in 1789 with a lighthouse running on new-fangled oil lamps and later equipped with two cannons to warn off any invasion by Napoleon.

Another two, erected in 1869, were superseded by Portland's current lighthouse in 1906.

Today's red and white striped construction is exactly how a lighthouse should look. On a clear day, its clean lines, dramatically outlined against an azure summer sky, are unforgettable.

Unfortunately, no whiskery lighthouse keeper recounting tall tales is in attendance as the lighthouse was automated in 1996.

An earlier incarnation

Two of its precursors can also be seen. One of them: the Old Higher Lighthouse, owned from 1923 to 1958 by birth control pioneer, Mary Stopes, even has cottages to rent.

Sturminster Newton has the perfect English mill, which perches picturesquely on the banks of the river Stour. The building's mellow brickwork reflects artfully in the glassy waters of the mill pond.

The mill has ground flour for Saxons, Normans and Plantaganets right up to 20thC and is open to the public throughout the summer months.

Visiting it you immediately sense in its dusty atmosphere that unbroken pedigree.

The rumble and clank of the wheel, vibrates through the entire building, making you wonder how it hasn't been shaken into the Stour years ago.

The mill's idyllic situation makes it a perfect picnic spot. While there are no facilities, there are picnic tables from which to take in this most quintessential of Dorset views.

Sandsfoot Castle

A short drive from the bustle of Weymouth lies an enchanted spot, Sandsfoot Castle and Gardens. Mostly the preserve of the locals, it has expansive views over Portland Harbour and Portland.

The castle ruins, artily perched on a low cliff next to the water's edge, aren't picturesque, though the setting makes up for this. It is one of two fortifications built by Henry VIII in 1547 at either side of Portland Harbour in response to the threat from Catholic Spain. (The other, Portland Castle is in much better condition and open to visit.)

Sandsfoot was constructed with stone taken from the newly dissolved abbeys at a cost of £4,000.00 (around £1.5 million today). It never saw action, and by the 17thC was a ruin, its stone robbed once again to build Weymouth Bridge. By 1930 it was deemed dangerous and was closed to the public.

With the aid of a Heritage Lottery grant it has been restored. Once again it is possible to wander among the remaining stone work and peer though gun ports checking for invading Spaniards as the defenders once did.

The old-fashioned municipal style gardens are a pleasant place to sit and sip tea at its tearoom.

A short walk downhill brings you to Castle Cove, again the preserve of a few locals, dog walkers or kayakers.

Castle Cove

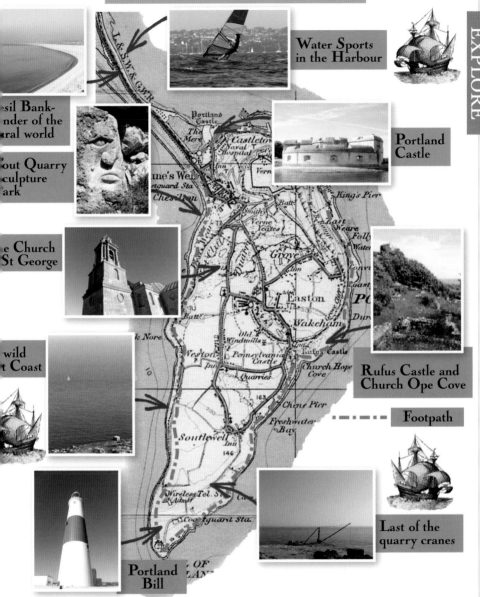

Water Sports
in the Harbour

Portland
Castle

...sil Bank-
...nder of the
...ral world

...out Quarry
...culpture
...ark

...e Church
...St George

...wild
...t Coast

Rufus Castle and
Church Ope Cove

Footpath

Last of the
quarry cranes

Portland
Bill

Portland has always been different: its people, its landscape, its traditions. Joined to the mainland by the merest sliver of shingle until 1839; its only connection with the mainland was by ferry. Bad weather meant it could be cut off for days.

The best way to experience this otherness is to pull on a pair of boots and walk its coastline. The route is about eight miles and well signposted.

Bridport has been rightly called the Notting Hill of Dorset and in keeping with this appellation it supports a number of lively markets. Apart from the usual street markets on Wednesday and Saturday, the town hosts a busy open air flea market on the last Sunday of the month, March just the right amount of tattiness. Even when there isn't a market, the area hosts a number of small antique and bric-a-brac shops where you can still find a bargain.

to September. This takes place on the St Michael's Trading Estate, which lies behind the High Street It is an atmospheric area distinctly unglamorous and with

Durlston Castle

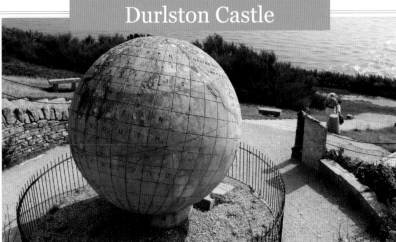

Durlston Country Park sits high on the Purbecks above Swanage. It possesses some of the best views, for the least amount of effort, in Dorset.

The Durlston Estate originally belonged to George Burt, native of Swanage,  who made his fortune working for his relative, John Mowlem, in London. If the surname sounds familiar it is because Uncle John founded Mowlems, one of the biggest Victorian civil contractors that survives to this day.

Burt dreamt of putting Swanage on the map by creating an upmarket housing development at Durlston. The centrepiece, Durlston Castle, was built with typical Victorian bravado in a mishmash of styles. Fortunately for us, the castle was the only part of the plan to be realised.

Burt also returned to Swanage with an eccentric collection of architectural antiques picked up from Mowlem developments in Victorian London. These he erected throughout Swanage. This also explains the cast-iron City of London bollards dotted about the castle grounds.

Durlston Castle has recently been carefully renovated and now acts as an interpretation centre and cafe.

The view from the cafe terrace is stunning, while below the castle rests Swanage's iconic stone globe also installed by Burt.

The cliff path winds on past the quaintly titled Tilly Whim Caves, in reality old quarry workings, now deemed unsafe to visit.

Lyscombe Chapel

Lyscombe Chapel hides in an unspoilt, hidden valley, its location unmarked, while the only way to reach it is on foot. It dates from the 13thC and was connected to the monastery of Milton Abbas. It was possibly used as a stopover for travelling monks, with the princely rent of 12 fishes being paid to the landowner.

Following the Dissolution, the chapel and accompanying priest's house became a bakehouse for several hundred years.

More recently it lay abandoned, doomed to crumble to nothingness until the endeavour of an enlightened landowner breathed life into it once again. The resulting restoration meant that in 2007 Mass was celebrated here for the first time in 500 years.

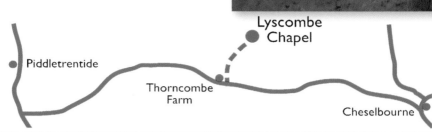

Lyscombe Chapel

Piddletrentide

Thorncombe Farm

Cheselbourne

Early on Christmas day 1839, inhabitants living close to the cliffs that lie between Lyme Regis and Seaton were awoken, not by carols, but by an unearthly rumble. Cottage walls cracked and fissures opened up, whilst below, the sea boiled as a wall of shingle rose up from the seabed.

At daybreak the effects were immediately apparent—eight million tons of rock along a seven mile stretch of coastline had slid seawards forming a huge chasm and a 15-acre island later known as Goat Island.

The superstitious blamed it on divine retribution though it was actually the result of geology and weeks of torrential rain. Waterlogged sandy upper layers of soils had slid beachward over the less permeable lower clay layers.

But there is no such thing as an ill wind. The event, which caused no casualties, caught the public imagination. The huge influx of sightseers were soon being charged for the privilege of viewing this new natural wonder. At harvest time a 1,000 people gathered to watch as two remaining fields of corn, still growing on the newly formed Goat Island, were ceremoniously reaped with golden sickles borne by four maidens dressed all in white. There was even a polka composed in celebration.

The Undercliff, now a nature reserve, is a tiny lost world that even possesses. its own microclimate. Vines drape the trees while the calls of myriad birds echoing though the green canopy make you feel as if you are stepping into a rainforest.

Walking the Undercliff is reasonably straightforward and starts at the far corner of the Cobb car park.

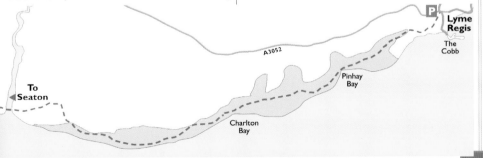

O nce upon a time there was a prince who dreamt of building a magical utopia: a town where harmony and proportion reigned for ever and ever.

The prince was called Charles, the town, Poundbury. Whether it is a fairytale, it provokes fierce debate especially when opinions are invariably coloured by attitudes to the man, strength of feeling.

Poundbury lies on the outskirts of Dorchester and is now in its 21st year. When completed in 2023 it will contain 2,500 new homes and a population of 5,000, increasing the population of Dorchester by a quarter.

From the beginning, the plan never aspired to be cutting edge.

The novel element of the scheme was far more subtle, to create a development where factories, private dwellings, social

rather than to his vision.

Given that his dream is so benign, it is strange that the project provokes such

housing and retail existed in harmony and car dependency was reduced.

Exploring Poundbury makes you appreciate just how ambitious the scheme is. In fact you can quite easily get lost amongst its streets and alleyways, which take inspiration from, rather than slavishly copying, existing architectural styles.

Between Poundbury and Maiden Castle a footpath conveniently meanders across the fields joining the spanking new settlement of Poundbury to the the rather more ancient one of Maiden Castle.

It is around 40 minutes each way with lots to interest at both ends, as well as a plethora of cafes at Poundbury.

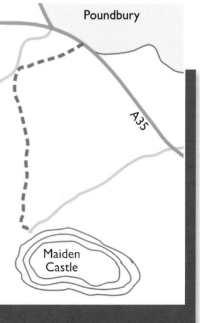

The lure of the beach means the Town Mill of Lyme Regis is an overlooked gem. Hidden in the back streets of the old town, it needs just that bit more effort to find.

Surrounding a cobbled courtyard, the working mill was first recorded in the Domesday Book and continued grinding away until 1926. It then remained empty and derelict until the inevitable plans to demolish and replace it with a car park in 1991 inspired enthusiastic residents to band together and restore it. The result of

10 year's dedication was finally unveiled by John Fowles in 2001.

Once more the wheel clunks, thunks and turns, vibrating the whole structure and making it feel like a living thing. Enthusiastic volunteer millers, meanwhile, explain the mysterious

processes that turn grain into flour. The rambling ancillary buildings are

occupied by small craft businesses and a cafe as well as hosting three galleries. Behind the mill buildings lies an intimate little garden based on the original layout.

The Cross and Hand complete with offerings from passing travellers

On a lonely hill above the village of Batcombe stands a humble chalk pillar. Even though its appearance is so unprepossessing, it has stood here since time immemorial. Its significance has been lost to history, while its name, the Cross and Hand, refers to no remaining visible decoration.

Theories abound: it could be a Medieval boundary marker or even Roman pillar from a villa.

The Cross and Hand also has literary pretentions, as Thomas Hardy gave it a walk-on role in his novel, *Tess of the D'Urbervilles.*

Tess's seducer Alec D'Urberville forces her to...

'put your hand on that stone hand and swear you will never tempt me by your charms or ways.'

It makes a focal point for a glorious off-road ride or walk best taken at drier times of the year (See P.16).

Batcombe

The Cross
and Hand

Minterne
Magna

A37

Maiden Castle

Maiden Castle, the largest Iron Age hill fort in Europe, occupies a low hill just a mile or so from the town of Dorchester, yet it still retains an atmosphere of lofty isolation. The towering defensive banks and ditches rise up like frozen waves and are a blissful place to lie back on a summer's day and listen to the cry of the invisible skylark high above.

To really appreciate the earthwork requires wings, only then can you understand the sophisticated defensive banks of this ancient structure.

It was here, 2,000 years ago, that the might of the Roman army, led by the future emperor Vespasian, met the local tribespeople, the Durnovaria, in a battle that was probably a forgone conclusion. British slingshots would have been no match for Rome's state-of-the-art ballistas.

The details of their last stand was revealed in chilling detail when Mortimer Wheeler, the archaeologist, conducted an extensive dig here some 70 years ago.

A mass grave of the defenders was uncovered, with the skeletons clearly exhibiting battle wounds, while huge reserves of sling stones brought from nearby Chesil Bank still lay unused.

Today life here is far more peaceful, the occupation force is mainly sheep, lambs and dog walkers while the hill's occupants have long ago forsaken their ancestral home for the bright lights of Dorchester town.

Roman shale ointment jar

There is a Dorset industry, at least as old as farming, stretching back in one form or another for many thousands of years

During the Iron Age, bituminous shale, which outcrops at Kimmeridge Bay, was carved and turned to produce decorative objects that have been found across the British Isles.

Evidence of this early bling once littered the beach in the form of discarded cores from worked shale known locally as Kimmeridge 'coal money.'

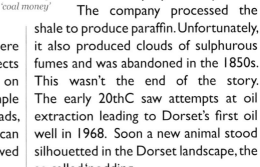

Kimmmeridge 'coal money'

With the arrival of the Romans, there were two 'factories' producing objects that have been found at sites on Hadrian's Wall. These vary from simple bracelets to gold studded mace heads, while in the County Museum can be found a delicately carved shale table leg.

With the departure of the Romans the shale that made locals look good now made them feel warm. The oil impregnated shale was used as fuel even though it produced highly toxic fumes.

Then in the 19thC shale jewellery experienced a revival. Cut and then polished with beeswax, it closely resembled jet, that black shiny stone beloved by Victorian jewellers.

During this period the further potential of this oil-bearing rock was recognised with the founding in 1848 of the catchily entitled 'Bituminous Shale Company' in Weymouth. The company processed the shale to produce paraffin. Unfortunately, it also produced clouds of sulphurous fumes and was abandoned in the 1850s. This wasn't the end of the story. The early 20thC saw attempts at oil extraction leading to Dorset's first oil well in 1968. Soon a new animal stood silhouetted in the Dorset landscape, the so called 'nodding donkey.' Dorset's first oil well, called 'Well One,' now extracts 28 million gallons of crude each year.

Shale table leg, Roman- County Museum

Lambert's Castle

Lambert's Castle is the site of an Iron Age fort, as are many of Dorset's high points, and until quite recent times the site of a yearly fair.

Nowadays it is stewarded by the National Trust and is a favourite with dog walkers, horse riders and kite flyers. The hill has two completely different flavours. On one side paths run through woodland glades composed of fantastically gnarled trees, whose cover of moss makes them glow a vibrant green in the morning sunlight. A great place for chasing hobbits into hollow trunks or white rabbits down holes and

a brilliant place for kids to have some real fun.

The other side is wide-open hillside with spectacular and far reaching views, encompassing most of Dorset. There are even seats from which to enjoy your flask of coffee while feeding your sandwiches to the passing mutts.

The First Crematorium

Standing in the peaceful village churchyard of Manston near Sturminster Newton is an elegant mausoleum which has a most interesting tale to tell.

It was here, in 1882 that a revolution in the British way of death began.

Six years earlier, the lord of the manor's first wife passed away with the dying wish that

Flame finial atop the the Mausoleum

her resting place would not be the flood-prone family vault. Her husband, Captain Hanham, therefore devised a novel solution to the problem— cremation.

Strange as it may seem, cremations had not taken place in Britain since Roman times and were in fact illegal. Because of this, it took six years to overcome all the obstacles and more importantly, to build a crematorium in the grounds of Manston Manor, which overlooks the churchyard.

The bodies of the Captain's first wife, and his third (who also happened to be his first wife's sister!) were placed in lead-lined coffins. An elegant classical mausoleum was built to contain them.

When all was finally ready the cremations were...

'carried out without the slightest unpleasantness to those who stood within two feet of the white flame and promptly resolved the bodies to harmless elements.'

In a typical Victorian fashion Hanham was moved to describe in detail the exact appearance and composition of the ashes...

"fragments of the (bone) looked like frosted silver and broke at the touch..."

He was obviously a convert as in 1883, he too was cremated in a new, improved crematorium. All three urns were then placed in this elegant mausoleum under the trees.

The crematorium still remains out of sight in the Manor grounds though now acts as a mundane garden shed.

Manston Mausoleum

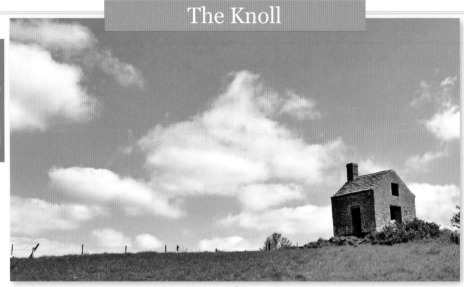

The coast road between Bridport and Abbotsbury consists of a multitude of magnificent views. Often overlooked is the Watchhouse, standing high on a hill above Bexington.

Swyre

The Knoll

West Bexington

B3175

Received wisdom says its purpose was as a fisherman's lookout for spotting the approach of shoals of fish. It's a romantic idea.

The tiny building is perfectly self-contained with even a little fireplace. The Knoll is easy to reach as long as you don't miss the turning. A few minute's scramble takes you to a thoughtfully placed bench at the foot of the little building.

The views are spectacular though the shoals of fish are long gone, served battered with chips, no doubt.

View of St Catherine's Chapel, Chesil Bank and Portland

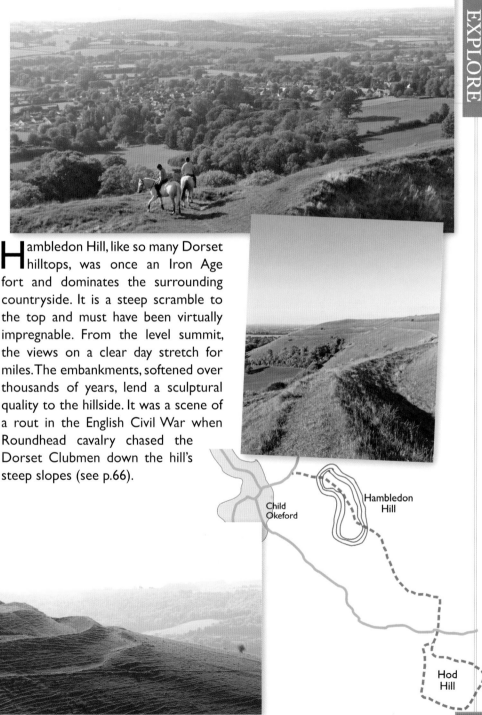

Hambledon Hill, like so many Dorset hilltops, was once an Iron Age fort and dominates the surrounding countryside. It is a steep scramble to the top and must have been virtually impregnable. From the level summit, the views on a clear day stretch for miles. The embankments, softened over thousands of years, lend a sculptural quality to the hillside. It was a scene of a rout in the English Civil War when Roundhead cavalry chased the Dorset Clubmen down the hill's steep slopes (see p.66).

Child Okeford

Hambledon Hill

Hod Hill

The Chained Library

Climbing a twisting spiral staircase in Wimborne Minster (see p.116) brings you to a 14thC room once the Minster treasury now home to one of the few remaining chained libraries in Britain.

It is chained because it was also Britain's first public library.

The collection, founded in 1686, was opened up to 'the better class of person' in 1695 to become, in effect, the first public library. The readers may have been better class, but no one was taking any chances, hence the chains. The books cover a wealth of subjects from gardening and etiquette to building.

Horton Tower

Starkly outlined against the open countryside, Horton Tower is a massive Gothic brick pile that celebrates nothing in particular. It was built in 1750 by the Lord of the Manor and part-time architect Humphrey Sturt and falls into that very English category of building–the Folly, and at 140 feet high, it's big.

Though reasons have been put forward as to the towers use, it remains to this day, an elegant enigma.

Horton

Horton Tower

Distance 8.5 miles
OS Explorer OL22

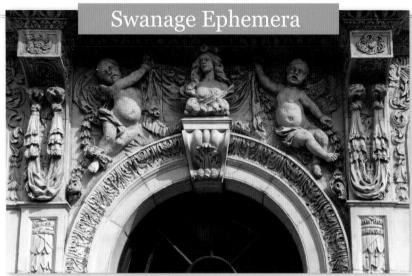

Town Hall facade from the Mercer's Hall, City of London

Dotted around Swanage are a number of rather incongruous pieces of street architecture, ranging from Doric columns to cast-iron lamp standards, mysteriously inscribed, 'St George Hanover Square'.

They owe their place in the town to John Mowlem and nephew John Burt, local Victorian entrepreneurs who founded the still extant Mowlem construction company. The business helped remodel 19thC London (see p.97), and in the process accumulated a wealth of architectural salvage that Molem and Burt had shipped back as ballast in returning stone ships to adorn the town. Most notable is the front of the town hall which incorporates a section of the facade of the old Mercer's Hall dating from the 17thC and attributed to the architect Christopher Wren.

Clock tower from London Bridge

Walking to the seafront you will find a clocktower. It originally stood on the approach to London Bridge commemorating the Duke of Wellington. It now lacks its original clock and Gothic spire. The choicest pieces though are to be found at George Burt's former home now the Purbeck House Hotel and range from Roman mosaic to statues from the Royal Exchange.

Doric columns of unknown provenance

Pilsdon Pen

The summit of Pilsdon Pen is the highest point in Dorset and provides a 360-degree view of the countryside, Like many Dorset hilltops, it was once including Bronze Age burial mounds, the remains of a medieval rabbit warren, and silhouetted against the skyline, another poignant relic of a bygone age, an Ordnance Survey trig point now consigned to history by the recent arrival of GPS.

an Iron Age hillfort. A lay-by just below the summit makes access easy.
Its hummocky crest has borne witness to various degrees of occupation,

The Sub-tropical Gardens

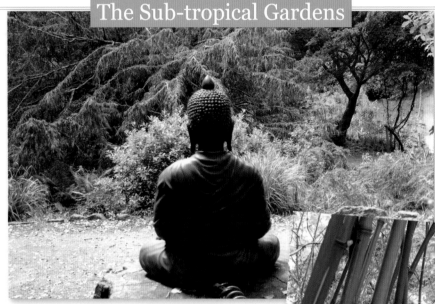

As the name suggests, the gardens at Abbotsbury take advantage of the micro-climate created by sheltering cliffs

and originated as the kitchen garden of Abbotsbury Castle, the summer

residence of the Countess of Ilchester. Her green fingers were passed through the generations until the carefully planned wilderness took shape.

While the gardens have gone from

strength to strength the Castle did not, burning to the ground in 1919 so that no trace now remains.

Standing on the Dorset/Somerset border is the tiny church of All Saints. It is lost at the end of a narrow lane a stone's throw from the pretty reservoir of Sutton Bingham, its humble exterior giving no hint of the riches hidden inside.

The interior is richly embellished with

Open belfry, lefthand bell was actually cast onsite in 14thC

medieval paintings dating from the 13thC and 14thC. They were whitewashed over during the reformation and only rediscovered in the 1860s.

The best paintings are on the north wall of the nave and show two scenes from the death of the Virgin, while above the beautifully preserved Norman chancel arch is a scene of the crowning of the Virgin. Painted figures even decorate the window reveals. It is a timeless place and especially precious when you realise that in the outside world such venerable art as this would be secure behind glass in a museum.

Wimborne Minster

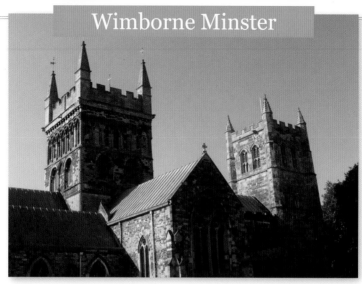

The Minster stands homely and squat in the centre of Georgian Wimborne, no soaring Gothic spires here. There was a spire, but it collapsed

Tomb of Margaret Beaufort, mother of Henry VII

400 years ago.

The fabric of the church is mainly Norman though the site is much older and has been renovated several times in the intervening centuries, including a very thorough renovation in the 1850s. Even so, there is still a lot to see,

including an ancient chained library and a colourful 14thC clock. Close to the altar lies the tomb of Margaret Beaufort mother of Henry VII and a benefactor of the Minster.

Small fragments of the pre-Reformation painting which would have originally embellished the church from wall to ceiling also remain.

In one wall is to be found the sarcophagus of eccentric Anthony Ettricke who decreed his burial place be neither in the open or under the church.

Sarcophagus of Anthony Ettericke

As a result he was buried half in and half out of the church. He was also convinced that he would draw his last breath in 1693. To his embarrassment he lasted another ten years meaning a last minute amendment to the coffin's inscription.

Medieval decoration

This church was once a place of medieval pilgrimage, the focus being the Anglo Saxon shrine of St Candida. This shrine is a rare pre-Reformation survival, the only other being that of Edward the Confessor in Westminster Abbey.

It is an unassuming, altar-like structure pierced by three oval cavities into which pilgrims would place their infected or injured limbs hoping for a cure.

The origins of St Candida herself are hazy, though repairs carried out in 1900 discovered the bones of a small woman of about 40 years and the inscription, 'Here lie the bones of St White'. Continuity is maintained to this very day with the three niches filled with parishioners' petitions requesting intervention from the saint.

Sir George Somers, a Lyme Regis sea captain who sailed from Plymouth to Virginia and on the way claimed Bermuda for England, has his memorial here. He liked his food as he died from consuming '*a surfeit of pig*' in 1610.

People still petition St Candida

Outside in the graveyard lie the remains of two famous political animals, Bulgarian dissident, Georgi Markov, famously assassinated by means of a poisoned-tipped umbrella on Waterloo Bridge and political broadcaster and interviewer, Sir Robin Day, whose memorial reads: '*In loving memory of Sir Robin Day—the Grand Inquisitor.*'

Bere Regis

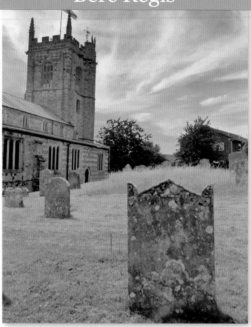

The church of St John the Baptist dates back to the years before the Norman invasion. It has strong connections with Thomas Hardy, whose novel, *Tess of the D'Urbervilles,* hinges on the fate of the D'Urbervilles. They huddle together in the vaults below this very church.

Its chief glory though, is the magnificent medieval roof—a mixture of bold carved roof bosses and near life-sized carvings of the apostles. It was given by Cardinal Morton in 1485, probably in memory of his parents. The roof is unique, though stylistically it has several parallels in Norfolk such as the famous corbels of Norwich Cathedral.

After looking up, look down.
On several of the pillars are medieval carvings which seem out of place in a church. Sufferers of toothache and headaches are among them.

Medieval depiction of headache

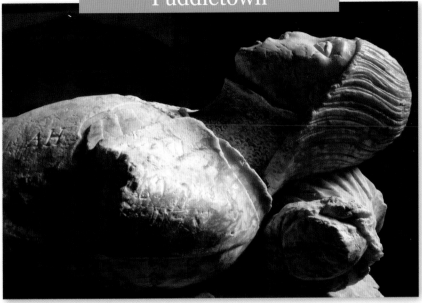

This church of St Mary the Virgin is closely associated with Thomas Hardy, in fact Puddletown features as Wetherbury in Hardy's novels.

It was here that many of his relations

Early 19thC fire buckets

worshipped and left their mark as graffiti in the church.

Dating from the late Middle Ages, the church's atmospheric interior houses a set of box pews complete with hooks for top hats as well as wall paintings, which were whitewashed over by the Puritans. There is also a wonderful group of marble tombs belonging to the Martyns of Athelhampton, dating from the 14thC and recently the subject of an extensive renovation project.

The church door was obviously the subject of potshots in the Civil War–lead pellets were dug out of it during conservation and are on display.

Finally, hanging in the gloom, are two items which demonstrate the pleasing eccentricity of church contents: canvas fire buckets dating from 1805, printed boldly with the name of their provider, Sun Insurance.

Chideock

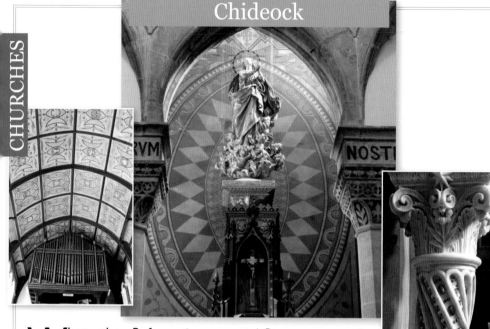

When the Reformation swept away the old religion, Chideock remained staunchly wedded to its Catholic traditions. As a result, seven local men were hung, drawn and quartered in Dorchester for their beliefs while an eighth died in prison. They became known as the Chideock Martyrs.

The Church of Our Lady Queen of Martyrs and St Ignasius, built in 1874, commemorates their deaths. It also incorporates the original barn that had long served the Catholic congregation as a chapel. Charles Weld, the Lord of the Manor, not only designed and built the new church but decorated much of the interior. The result, based on the Italian Romanesque, has been described as a gem of Catholicism. The church houses a varied collection of relics, including a fragment of the true cross as well as a small museum of local history. A short walk across the fields takes you to a tall wooden cross, again commemorating the martyrs and stands on the site of Chideock Castle This was the scene of bitter fighting during the Civil War and eventually demolished by the Parliamentarians.

Chideock Martyrs memorial on the site of Chideock Castle

North Chideock

Church of Our Lady Queen of Martyrs

Chideock Martyr's Cross and Site of Chideock Castle

Church of St Giles

Chideock   A35

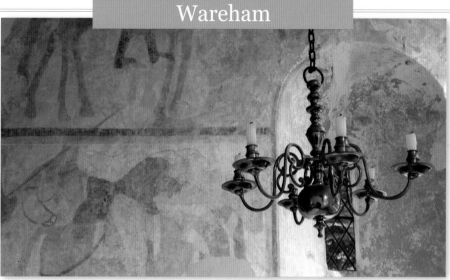

The church of St Martin's is worth a visit for several reasons.

Firstly, it is the only example of a Saxon church in Dorset that survives close to its original state. As in most early churches, the focus is the altar, round which the Mass was celebrated. Indeed, the altar takes up a big chunk of the church. The tall, narrow nave as well as a tiny window in the north side of the chancel are original, dating back to 1030, while in the northwest aisle is Saxon wall arcading and a Saxon door. Next, there are the 12thC frescoes on the north wall of the chancel depicting St Martin on horseback dividing his cloak to give one half to a beggar.

Finally, the church is home to a life-sized recumbent effigy of T. E. Lawrence in full Arab dress (see p.48-49). His friend Eric Kennington, the official war artist for the First and Second World Wars, carved it out of Purbeck marble and Portland stone. Lawrence is portrayed wearing an Arab headdress and holding camel whips as well as two books: *The Greek Anthology of Verse* & *The Oxford Book of English Verse* and a dagger given to him by Prince Faisal.

The monument was originally intended for St Pauls who rejected it as did both Westminster Abbey and Salisbury Cathedral. It was their loss as around 10,000 visitors a year come to the church just to see the sculpture.

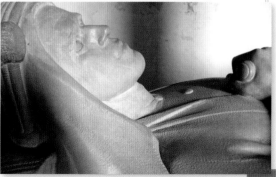

Monument to T.E Lawrence
by Eric Kannington

A FEW WORDS ABOUT MAPS

It's amazing how many people set off to walk or cycle without a good map. Apart from the obvious... you get lost...they are an absolute treasure trove of information about the countryside you're passing through; even if they aren't quite detailed enough to show the cows in the fields, the largest scale do show the actual fields. For this book I've relied on Ordnance Survey maps–1:50,000 is fine for on-road cycling while the 1:25,000 is most suitable for walking and off-road cycling.

The Ordnance Survey has moved into the digital age and now includes a digital download with each map purchased.

Invaluable if you walk or cycle a lot are *OS Maps* digital maps. Less than £20 buys you a year's subscription to all OS maps online. This enables you to plan your own walks and download them to the OS GPS phone app. Then you have little reason to get lost.

Another excellent free app, *Viewranger,* offers a similar facility, but relies on 'open source' maps–not quite as detailed but perfectly usable. You can also purchase OS maps for use through the *Viewranger* app.

Another useful feature of the app is their *'buddy beacon,'* which lets others see exactly where you are.

To err is human

All constructive comments gratefully received
idicks@icloud.com

Thanks to:
Advantage Digital Print 01305 757472
Margaret Chamberlain, Tilly Lavenas and Guy Ottewell for proofreading

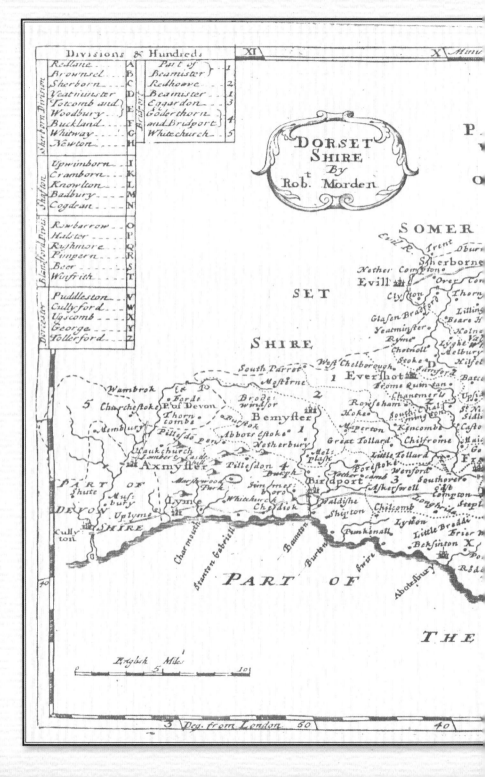

| Divisions & Hundreds | | | | XI | | X | Minu |

Sherborn Division	Redlane	A
	Brownsel	B
	Sherborn	C
	Yeatminster	D
	Totcomb and Woodbury	E
	Buckland	F
	Whitway	G
	Newton	H

Bridport	Part of Beaminster	1
	Redhoave	2
	Beaminster	1
	Eggardon	3
	Goderthorn and Bridport	4
	Whitchurch	5

Shafton	Upwimborn	I
	Cramborn	K
	Knowlton	L
	Badbury	M
	Cogdean	N

Blandford Dirit	Rowbarrow	O
	Halster	P
	Rushmore	Q
	Pimpern	R
	Beer	S
	Winfrith	T

Dorcester	Puddleston	V
	Cullyford	W
	Ugscomb	X
	George	Y
	Tollerford	Z

DORSET
SHIRE
By
Rob. Morden

P.
O

SOMER

SET

SHIRE

Evill R. Trent Oburn
Nether Compton Sherborne
Evill Over Con
Clyston Thorn
Lillins
Glasen Bradford Beare H
Yeatminster Holne
Ryme Lighe Val
Chetnoll Melbury
Stoke D Hilfet
West Chelborough Tarsford Batc
South Parret 1 Evershott
Mosterne Frome Quintan Upsi
Chantmerl St N
Brode windsor 2 Rowsham Sidli
Eel 10 Hoke South Chal Casto
P. of Devon Buttok Bemyster Mcperton Kincomb Mais
Thorn Abbots Estoke 1 Great Tollard Chilfrome Ge
comb Netherbury Little Tollard Fra
Pillesdo Pen Melplash Porestoke Wonsford
Haukchurch Forde Lamberts Castle Pillesdon 4 Nethercomb Southover
Axmyster Burgh Birdport 3 East
Marshwood Simsmes boro Askerswell Compton
Park Waldishe Longbrid Stepl
Lyme Whitchurch Shipton Chilcomb
Uplyme Chediok Lyston Little Braddi
Punkenall Frier Ma
Charmouth Beunton Behsinton X
Burton Abotsbury Rdd

PART OF DEVON SHIRE

PART OF THE

English Miles

Part of Devon
Thute
Mus bury
Cullyton
Wambrok
Charchestoke
Hembury
5

3 Deg. from London 50 40